The Return
of the
Ragpicker

Other Bantam Books by Og Mandino

THE GREATEST SALESMAN IN THE WORLD
THE GREATEST SALESMAN IN THE WORLD,
  PART II: The End of the Story
THE GREATEST MIRACLE IN THE WORLD
THE GREATEST SUCCESS IN THE WORLD
THE GIFT OF ACABAR (*with Buddy Kaye*)
THE CHRIST COMMISSION
THE CHOICE
OG MANDINO'S UNIVERSITY OF SUCCESS
MISSION: SUCCESS!
A BETTER WAY TO LIVE

The Return of the Ragpicker

Og Mandino

BANTAM BOOKS

NEW YORK • TORONTO • LONDON • SYDNEY • AUCKLAND

For Matt and Lori Mandino
with Love

THE RETURN OF THE RAGPICKER
A Bantam Book / March 1992

All rights reserved.
Copyright © 1992 by Og Mandino.
No part of this book may be reproduced or transmitted
in any form or by any means, electronic or mechanical,
including photocopying, recording, or by any information
storage and retrieval system, without permission in
writing from the publisher.
For information address: Bantam Books.

Library of Congress Cataloging-in-Publication Data

Mandino, Og.
    Return of the ragpicker / Og Mandino.
        p.   cm.
    ISBN 0-553-07129-7
    1. Success.   2. Conduct of life.   I. Title.
BJ1611.2.M3245   1992
158'.1—dc20   91-35078
                                                            CIP

Published simultaneously in the United States and Canada

Bantam Books are published by Bantam Books, a division of Bantam
Doubleday Dell Publishing Group, Inc. Its trademark, consisting of the
words "Bantam Books" and the portrayal of a rooster, is Registered in
U.S. Patent and Trademark Office and in other countries. Marca
Registrada. Bantam Books, 666 Fifth Avenue, New York, New York
10103.

PRINTED IN THE UNITED STATES OF AMERICA
BVG   0 9 8 7 6 5 4 3 2 1

We are born for a higher destiny than that of earth. There is a realm where the rainbow never fades, where the stars will be spread out before us like islands that slumber on the ocean and where the beings that now pass before us, like shadows, will stay in our presence forever.

BULWER-LYTTON

A Special Message from Og Mandino

━━━━━━━━━━━━━━━━━━━━━━━━━━━━━━━━━━━━━━

The mysterious old ragpicker, Simon Potter, who disappeared at the end of my book, *The Greatest Miracle in the World* . . .

Did I ever expect to be writing about him again, in some future book?

For more than fifteen years, my response to hundreds of interviewers and thousands of letters was always the same . . . "not likely."

And so, you are now holding a book that I had never planned to write. If life is a series of surprises, as Emerson wrote, then the book you are about to read certainly ranks as a major surprise in a career that has been filled with them.

During the past quarter century my life has also been blessed with more good fortune and honors than any human being deserves.

I have shared both hunger and wealth, pain and joy with the woman I love by my side, and I have watched proudly as my two sons grew to manhood, married happily, and embarked on promising careers.

I have been inducted into the International Speakers Hall of Fame, received the Napoleon Hill Gold Medal for literary excellence, and read my biography, with pride, in *Who's Who in the World*.

Most important was the fulfillment of my childhood dream and that of my late, beloved mother . . . to become a writer. That I stumbled along life's often-rutted highways, plus a gutter or two, until I had passed the age of forty before reaching our cherished goal, was my fault and mine alone.

In retrospect, those early years of failure, despair, and poverty were far more valuable than any college education could have been. Since 1966, the fourteen books I have written, all dealing with the true meaning of success and happiness and how to capture those two elusive songbirds, have managed to sell more than twenty-five million copies in eighteen languages, from Tokyo to Rome, from Johannesburg to Sydney, from Mexico City to Stockholm! And one of them, *The Greatest Salesman in the World*, has ascended to especially rarified atmosphere by becoming the best-selling book of *all time*, in the *entire world*, in the field of sales! Dream fulfilled!

And yet, despite all those book sales and all the attention that *The Greatest Salesman*, both *Part I* and *Part II*, has received through the years, another of my books, *The Greatest Miracle in the World*, has consistently generated far more mail, since its publication in 1975, than all the other works combined!

The Greatest Miracle in the World is the story of my special friendship with a long-haired, giant old man, Simon Potter, who called himself a rag-picker because he spent all his time rescuing humans who had ended up on life's refuse pile. Our accidental first meeting was in the dingy parking lot behind my office building, during the years when I headed *Success Unlimited* magazine in Chicago, and soon I was stopping by his tiny, book-filled apartment across the street almost nightly before driving to my suburban home. Over several memorable months he shared his sherry, his wisdom, and his compassion with me, and his kindly advice and counsel changed my life forever . . . for the better. Then, one morning, he vanished without a trace. Amazingly, no one living in his apartment building recognized or admitted to knowing the old man from my description, even including the family residing in what had been *his* apartment, which they insisted they had occupied for four years! It was almost as if Simon had never existed . . . *except to me!* His parting gift, discovered later on my desk, was a powerful piece he had written called "The God Memorandum," a document containing four principles one must follow in order to enjoy a more fulfilling life. I shared the "Memorandum" with all my readers in the book . . . and they responded!

The essence of their messages to me in what has continued, through the years, to be a never-ending avalanche of letters about *The Greatest Miracle*, is best contained in the following few excerpts from actual letters received:

"Just one year ago, at this time, I was preparing to commit suicide. Your words, and those of your friend, the ragpicker in *Greatest Miracle*, saved my life. Today, I can honestly tell anyone that I am a miracle. Not just to be sober, but alive. Today I have serenity and joy in my life and your words helped carry me through all my days of hell. . . ."

"I owe you so much. In the summer of '83, shortly after my divorce, I sat on a California beach reading *The Greatest Miracle in the World* with tears rolling down my cheeks. You and that wonderful ragpicker, Simon Potter, were my life support. . . ."

"For the past twelve years I have been working with dependent, neglected, and delinquent boys, ages ten to seventeen, so I have been able to be one of God's ragpickers, like Simon Potter in your precious book. . . ."

"I am writing to express my gratitude to you for the inspiration and love you project in all of your books. I turn to *The Greatest Miracle in the World* whenever I get down on myself. I need only read those magnificent words to know that I can make it through any crisis and often I will give copies to friends who are burdened with life's problems. . . ."

"I am only 12 and already my life felt like it was coming apart. Thank you very much for your book about the old ragpicker. I think I got my life back together now, with the help of your book, and almost all the people I know like me. This makes me feel really good. . . ."

"I shall remember the ragpicker forever. . . ."

An old Texas friend, praising my work several years ago over dinner, proudly announced that he had finally discovered the secret to my success. He said I had reinvented the parable . . . those precious short fictitious stories of old that always illustrated a moral attitude or religious principle. He was probably closer to the truth than all the book reviews.

Did the old ragpicker, Simon Potter, ever actually exist, or was that story, too, a modern parable like so many of my other books? To all those who have raised that question, in one form or another, either during radio, television, or newspaper interviews or in letters, my response has always been and always will be the same, "Turn to John 4:48."

Then said Jesus unto him, Except ye see signs and wonders, ye will not believe.

There has never been, nor will there ever be, any follow-up explanation . . . either for *The Greatest Miracle in the World* or for this sequel that you are now holding.

Whether your first encounter with Simon Potter was in *The Greatest Miracle in the World*, many years ago, or still lies in the pages ahead, I welcome you with a loving embrace plus a gentle whisper in your ear. Please waste none of your precious time searching any New Hampshire map for the town of Langville, the setting for this book, because you will seek in vain. Out of respect for the proud, stubborn, and hard-working Yankee townspeople who have a tough enough time tolerating "summer folks," much less "curiosity seekers," I have altered the descriptions of all easily identifiable landmarks as well as changed the name of that lovely green and granite hamlet that is the locale of my story.

By the time you have read the final sentence on the last page of this volume, it is my fervent hope that you, too, will sigh a little and say . . .

"I shall remember the ragpicker forever. . . ."

Who could ask for more?

OG MANDINO
New Hampshire

The Return
of the
Ragpicker

The old man sat back on the stone wall and patted my knee gently. "Mister Og, it is not mere chance that has reunited us after all our years apart. We have been brought together for some special purpose, and since we are all instruments of heaven, I am convinced that you] have been led here, not by chance but in answer to my prayers. . . .

I

It is never easy to turn back the clock. It is almost impossible to turn back the calendar. Almost.

As she has done so often during our many years together, Bette was probably reading my mind. While she skillfully guided the long and luxurious vehicle through heavy traffic, she smiled and said, "Well, husband, how do you like riding in your first time machine?"

Her question didn't even surprise me. I just patted her knee and replied, "So far, so good, lady. I'm glad I listened to you."

"Me too!"

It was dusk but the sky was still smudged with stubborn streaks of pink and copper as we headed north on Route 93 toward the New Hampshire border. Bette was driving the blue Lincoln Town Car we had just rented at Boston's Logan Airport following our long flight from Phoenix.

For the most part we rode in silence even when familiar landmarks from the past flashed by on what was turning into a unique journey with another dimension for both of us. Thomas Wolfe had once written a very powerful novel stressing the theme that none of us can ever recapture our yesterdays by going home again, but after more than thirty years Bette and I were finally returning for a brief visit to that special part of New England where we had met, fallen in love, married, and commenced our life together.

It had all started over lunch one day, when I casually mentioned to Bette that our friend, Cheryl Miller, who has been my only agent for all my speaking engagements through the years, had just booked me for a speech at Boston's Hynes Convention Center in late June.

"Perfect!" she exclaimed. "I'm coming with you on that one."

I looked up, surprised. She rarely accompanied me on any of my speaking assignments unless the setting was an especially exotic one.

"I didn't say Bermuda or Sydney or Acapulco, hon. This speech is in Boston."

"I heard you . . . and I'm coming."

"Why?"

"Why? Why, you ask? Don't you remember the promise you made to our sons at Christmas last year?"

I didn't remember.

"Og, during those years when Dana and Matt were growing up, first in Illinois and then Arizona, we were always talking about taking them back to see Langville and some of the other New Hampshire places that have special memories for us. Well, it never happened. There was always a Disney World or that cottage in Michigan on Whitehall Lake or Little League playoffs that claimed priority on vacation time. And later, after the guys had gone off to college and then married, the possibility of our ever returning as a family grew very remote. Still, those two have always been fascinated by our stories and descriptions of that peaceful and lovely land where it all started for us."

"Now I remember my promise. Last Christmas when I opened that gift from both of them and it was the Sony camcorder I had been wanting more than anything else, neither of them were very subtle with their suggestions that perhaps I might use my new adult toy, soon, to videotape for them some of the places with special meaning, as well as a few landmarks, where you and I spent our first years together."

My wife mockingly applauded and said, "Well, here's our golden opportunity, author! You're scheduled to speak in Boston on Saturday. . . ?"

I nodded. "Saturday morning . . . ten to eleven or so."

"Okay. We'll fly into the city on Tuesday, rent a car, drive up north and give your camcorder a real workout for three days, hopefully capturing lots of our yesterdays on tape. I'll be your narrator. You can photograph while I stand by your side and tell the boys what they're viewing. How's that?"

I shook my head. "I don't know. After all these years, Langville could be a big letdown for us and a sorry disappointment for the boys when they finally get a look at the places we've been describing so glowingly for as long as they can remember. When it comes to our past, we humans all seem to let the bad memories fade away and inflate the happy moments. Maybe we should just let that part of our life and our world rest in peace . . . a nice fairy tale and love story that really did come true, thank God!"

Bette knew exactly how to deal with me. "Through the years, Og, we've been pretty good about keeping any promises we made to the boys."

What could I say? I reserved two round-trip tickets to Boston.

That first evening in New Hampshire we slept in a Ramada Inn on downtown Concord's Main Street. On the following morning, after breakfast, we walked just a few blocks and commenced our travelogue into the past on the grounds of the state capitol by photographing four old larger-than-life friends who hadn't aged a bit since we had last walked among them. First there was the towering granite statue of Colonel (and later, General) John Stark who had led the New Hampshire contingent at Bunker Hill and also authored the state motto, "Live free or die." Then there was Daniel Webster, senator, secretary of state, and the most eloquent man of his time; John Hale, minister to Spain, senator, abolitionist; and Franklin Pierce, fourteenth president of the United States. I turned toward the capitol building itself and panned up the graceful columns to its glowing gold tower while Bette, who had done her homework, announced that here was the oldest state capitol in the nation where the legislature still held its meetings in the original chambers. I added that Concord was one of our nation's smallest state capitals with a population of only slightly more than thirty thousand!

By the time we checked out of the Ramada Inn and drove slowly down Main Street, we were both in a semidaze. "Nothing has changed, Og," Bette whispered. "More than thirty years have passed and nothing has changed! Oh, the names on some of the stores are different and they could still use a good coat of paint, but the skyline seems to be about the same and the old red-brick buildings still have faded painted signs on their sides as always. It's all just as unspoiled and down-to-earth as it was when we used to take Dana shopping in his little stroller. I can't believe this!"

We drove to Oak Street and photographed the still-gray old Victorian building that had contained our first small apartment immediately after we were married. Then we went down to South Main and shot the now-shuttered Capitol Theatre, whose double-feature movies had been just about the only entertainment we could afford. Before that long and nostalgia-filled day had ended, we had also videotaped Shaker Village in Canterbury Center, Newfound Lake, where Bette and I had picnicked often, and Echo Lake with regal Franconia Notch reflected clearly in its glassy surface.

On Thursday we tried to capture the flavor of New Hampshire's only seaport, Portsmouth, as we had remembered it. Not difficult. The old Georgian mansions continued to stand proudly and majestically on tree-lined streets leading

5

down to the ocean, where weary tugboats were still bobbing in the cove near Ceres Street. Then we journeyed to Hampton Beach, just for a hot dog and soft drink, removed our tennis shoes and socks, and walked in the white sand, inhaling the tangy salt air once again. There were tears in Bette's eyes when we finally headed west, and on the way to Peterborough she sighed, "I had truly forgotten how lovely and peaceful and uncrowded and unphony it all is here. I guess it wasn't so easy to appreciate this state's many good qualities back then when we were struggling so hard just to pay the rent each week."

I leaned closer to her. "Do you remember the amount?"

She bit her lower lip and nodded. "Fifteen dollars."

Later I panned my camcorder slowly around Peterborough's downtown business district and bench-lined common while Bette's narration explained that Thornton Wilder had drawn on that town's setting for his classic drama, *Our Town*. By the time we arrived in Keene we were weary but still found enough energy to videotape each other waving and smiling as we walked through our favorite covered bridge on the Ashuelot River before checking into the Winding Brook Lodge for food and sleep. Getting fed was easy but sleeping was difficult. So many of the feature players, melodies, faces, and words that were our companions in those earlier New Hampshire years kept intruding on my slumber . . . John F. Kennedy, Arnold Palmer, *Gigi*, Floyd Patterson, Dwight D. Eisenhower, Chubby Checker, *The Sound of*

Music, J. D. Salinger, Sugar Ray Robinson, Khrushchev, *Exodus*, Charles Van Doren, *Goldfinger*, Mickey Mantle, *The Agony and the Ecstasy* . . .

On the following morning as we headed for our final destination, Langville; my humming camcorder was aimed through the front windshield of the rented Lincoln as we rode the curving and hilly two-lane paved road, bordered by stone walls, ferns, and wildflowers. Bette was narrating and in good voice, blending many of the facts she already knew about her hometown with fresh information she had acquired from all the New Hampshire travel and tourist literature she had received from our old friends, Cecil and Flossie White, who lived in nearby Chichester.

According to Bette, Langville's population had been approximately twelve hundred in 1930, and she estimated that, at most, it had doubled in the past sixty years. The town, she said, had five cemeteries, four churches, three filling stations, two restaurants, and one grocery store. Not bad ratios, she thought. On the east side of the Carlyle River that divided the small downtown area, there had once been a furniture manufacturing plant but since the Second World War, all business, both commercial and municipal, was conducted on less than a half mile of Main Street. We parked on that street, outside the old red-brick public library, and sat silently holding hands.

"Same as in Concord, Og," Bette said in a hushed voice. "It's just as if we drove away from here yesterday morning instead of so many years ago. The names on some of the stores are different

but that's all. The buildings . . . the colors . . .
the sounds . . . exactly as we left everything."

With my camcorder running, we walked
slowly past the Langville Inn, Robert's Hardware
Store, an old empty colonial that Bette explained
had once housed the telephone company's office,
and a two-story wooden building that contained
the town hall, selectmen's office, post office, and
police station. Then we crossed the street to the
Langville Savings Bank with its huge exterior
sign announcing that contributions were being
accepted, inside, for the new town ambulance.

I aimed the camcorder east along Main Street
and with the help of the zoom lens photographed
homes from five architectural periods, colonial,
Cape, Federal, Georgian, and Victorian, all looking like they were waiting to be acquired by
wealthy retirees from city life and converted into
bed-and-breakfast hideaways. We had, indeed,
moved through a time tunnel, and we were filled
with both joy and melancholy.

Back in the car, we drove to the large home on
Jefferson Avenue where my wife had spent her
childhood. Then I photographed the large white
clapboard building, now an apartment house,
where Bette had attended school for twelve years,
graduating in a class of eleven. Since she had
been a member of the Grange we also had to drive
up Bear Hill to get a good shot of Grange Hall,
where she had spent so many happy hours doing
good for others.

We returned to Main Street, parked, and
walked across the street to the church grounds,
complete with geranium beds and Civil War me-

morial, for the planned climactic closing scene of our videotape. After a lot of fussing, I finally had an image in the viewfinder that looked great. The tall, white spire of the stately old church was perfectly framed by a background of full, dark maples, and behind them the cloudless sky was powder blue. Bette stood close by, her right hand resting on my shoulder.

"We're just about finished, lady," I said, without removing my right eye from the viewfinder.

"I sure hope so," Bette said, sounding a little hoarse. "We must have more footage by now than *War and Remembrance.*"

"Ready?"

"Roll 'em, Spielberg!" she sighed.

I pressed the trigger-like shutter release as Bette leaned closer to the camera and its tiny microphone.

"Well, kids, we probably should have Streisand singing 'The Way We Were' behind this precious scene because you are now looking at that very special church, here in Langville, where your dad and I were married, on a cold and blustery December evening, a long, long time ago. You two were also christened here, although by the time you came along, Matt, we were living in Illinois because your father was running W. Clement Stone's magazine, *Success Unlimited*, although he still hadn't written his first book. It was a long drive back here for your christening, Matt, but it was worth it to have all our earliest and most important family roots originating on this same lovely village green. . . ."

Bette squeezed my shoulder and I stopped photographing. Tears were running down her cheeks again. She inhaled deeply and said, "I'm okay, hon, let's wrap this up."

"Follow me," I said and we both approached the tall war memorial that had been erected on the grounds in 1892. I focused, as clearly as I could, on the bronze tablet beneath the proud soldier:

IN MEMORY OF THE MEN OF LANGVILLE, WHO ON LAND AND SEA FOUGHT FOR LIBERTY, UNION AND EQUAL RIGHTS FOR ALL MANKIND, AND GAVE THEIR LIVES THAT FUTURE GENERA-TIONS MIGHT ENJOY THE BENE-FITS THEREOF.

"So there you are, guys," Bette said hesitantly. "Now you've seen some of New Hampshire as well as our old neighborhoods and maybe you understand, at last, why we loved it here so much. Both your dad and I hope that you have enjoyed this trip down memory lane with us as much as we have enjoyed putting it all together for you. We love you. God bless you both!"

The bell in the church steeple suddenly commenced tolling the noon hour. My Boston speech was scheduled for ten the following morning. We turned to each other but neither spoke as we walked slowly and reluctantly back to the car. Earlier we had decided that in order to avoid some of the late-afternoon traffic congestion surrounding Boston, we would start our two-hour journey south immediately after lunch.

Those *were* our plans. . . .

II

"Yellow birch!"

"Ash!"

"Peach!"

There was an unusual quality and pitch in her trembling voice that I had never heard before, a blending of joy and yearning, surprise and sadness, little girl and woman, wistfulness and anticipation.

"Sumac!"

"Red maple!"

I was fairly certain that I knew what Bette was doing, and so I remained silent as she drove slowly through a densely wooded section of Langville following our lunch in the town's only sit-down restaurant, overlooking the meandering Carlyle River. She had once told me that a favorite game of her childhood, usually played with her Uncle Bill whenever she rode in his pickup, was to see how many different types of trees they could identify as they rode along. Now my wife was not only performing on the stage of her youth again, she was also obviously fighting very hard to prevent the curtain from falling.

We had followed a gray tarred street leading out of the small downtown area that would eventually put us on the interstate turnpike south to Boston. The bumpy road wandered casually through the quiet countryside, passing a lonely white farmhouse every now and then, each with its own slumping or tilting nearby barn direly in need of paint. Climbing gradually, we finally reached a fork in the road and turned onto the left branch displaying a street sign that read Old Pound Road.

Bette gestured ahead. "You never got to see this part of my town when we were here more than thirty years ago, did you?"

"I don't think so. At least nothing is familiar. And this road we're on . . . Old Pound Road. What's an 'old pound'?"

"You'll never guess. Wait till you see it. Who knows, it might be something you can use in a book someday."

I sighed and raised my left wrist in an exaggerated move to check the time on my Omega.

"Don't worry, Og!" Now she sounded annoyed. "We'll be on the way to your precious Boston very soon. They're not expecting us till tonight, so there's still plenty of time. Just sit back and relax for the next few minutes while I help you solve the mystery of Old Pound Road."

I leaned toward her and kissed her cheek. Then I lowered my passenger window, raised the camcorder, and began photographing the lush fairyland of color and shadow to my right. Bright sunlight was sifting in gentle columns of pale gold down through the canopy formed by a variety of trees that were fenced in by ivy and moss-covered granite boulders, stacked two or three high, bordering both sides of the narrow road.

With the camera still running, I said, "Bette, I had forgotten how many stone walls there are back here in New England."

"Are you ready for a super piece of trivia?"

"Shoot!"

"I remember my dad telling me that long ago some Langville politician had estimated there were more than a thousand miles of stone walls in this town alone and the old boy had considered that quite an accomplishment since the Great Wall of China is only two thousand miles long!"

I shook my head in wonder. "Amazing. It would take two strong men to lift most of the stones and yet thousands of them were dug out of fields and meadows and fitted onto these walls, long before there were gas-powered tractors and loaders, by families who just had to stake out their own little corner of this world. What a tough group!"

Suddenly Bette hit the brake pedal hard enough so that I was grateful I had remembered to buckle up. After coming to a noisy stop, she shifted into reverse, backed slowly for perhaps twenty feet, and turned off the ignition.

"The trees have grown so tall and the bushes are now so thick along the road that I almost missed it," she said as she opened her door and stepped out. When I joined her, she put her arm around me and said, "This is your 'old pound,' Og. As you can see, it's just another granite stone wall, three feet or so high, but this section of the wall also has sides of approximately the same height that extend back perhaps forty feet to a rear wall, forming a square, with an opening back

13

there that one can walk through. Also, see how the inside area has been excavated so that it is perhaps two feet lower than this ground we're standing on."

On a large, flat-faced boulder, directly in front of us, was a bronze plaque darkened by age to a green patina that read

TOWN POUND BUILT 1817
RESTORED 1948
BY
LIZZY SIDES CHAPTER
DAUGHTERS
OF THE
AMERICAN REVOLUTION

"Almost two hundred years ago," Bette continued, now sounding like a tour guide, "this area was the center of the village and the townspeople erected this pound for everyone's benefit. Usually a pound, as you know, is an enclosure of some sort for housing stray or unlicensed animals. Well, this old stone corral, which is actually what it is, did just about that. If one's cattle wandered away from the old homestead or pasture, whoever retrieved them would bring them down here, lead them through that opening back there, and then roll a few heavy stones up against it so that the animals wouldn't escape. Later, when the owner of the livestock discovered his loss, this pound would always be the first place checked. Don't you think it looks great, considering its age? And obviously the town or some interested group is constantly working to keep the enclosure itself free of brush and leaves and aluminum cans. Og? Og, are you all right?"

"I'm okay," I replied, inhaling deeply.

Bette frowned and stepped closer, peering up into my eyes. "You look pale."

"I'm fine. Just experiencing that same old and familiar sensation. I never really know how to describe it . . . awe . . . wonder . . . vibrations of some sort, if you will, that always seem to hit me whenever I'm near a meaningful piece of the past. Whitman once said it was an instinct peculiar to artists and writers and composers. I don't know. You've seen me go through this many times before . . . when we walked beneath the ceiling of the Sistine Chapel, lit a candle in the Cathedral of Notre Dame, picked a blade of grass from the eighteenth fairway at St. Andrews, climbed those narrow steps to Anne Frank's tiny hideaway in Amsterdam, stood as close as we could to van Gogh's 'Vase with Sunflowers,' and stared, with tears in our eyes, at the squalid remains of the Mamertine Prison in Rome where Peter and Paul spent their last hours on earth. I can't explain it, hon, and I've never found anyone who could. Maybe I just overreact and the adrenaline gets pumping and that produces this slight electric shock sensation. I don't know. I just don't know."

"And you're feeling it here?" Bette asked incredulously. "You're picking up some kind of vibrations standing close to this old pound?"

"Yes, and that date on the plaque when this was built . . . another jolt!"

"Why? What's with 1817?"

I grinned and shook my head. "You know how

bad I've always been on dates. I'd miss everyone's birthday if it weren't for you and I'd miss yours, as well as our anniversary, if your mother didn't always remind me. And yet the year 1817 has a special place in my heart."

Bette shrugged helplessly. "Okay . . . I give up."

"My favorite author of all time? The one person whose writings and ideas I always turn to whenever I want to escape from the outside world and find myself again? The mentor who convinced me with his words and his example that a walk in the silent pines was worth far more than receiving a standing ovation from thousands . . . ?"

"Thoreau?"

"During the same year they were building this pound, the man whose philosophy about life has had the greatest influence on my thinking, except Christ, Henry David Thoreau, was born only about sixty miles south of here in that other Concord . . . the one in Massachusetts."

Bette put her hand over her mouth and remained silent. I leaned forward and gently rubbed a small moss-covered stone resting on top of the wall, thinking about how often in my writings and speeches I had insisted that God was always playing chess with us . . . making moves in our life and then sitting back to see how we would react to them. Was this one of God's moves? Instead of speeding down Everett Turnpike right now on the way to Massachusetts, why were we on this quiet country road visiting an old animal refuge and a boulder that bore Thoreau's birthday year? Coincidence? Or was it just the author in me overdramatizing an otherwise ordinary incident? I squeezed my wife's arm gently and said, "Thank you for showing me this precious relic of Langville's past."

As we were returning to our car, Bette suddenly exclaimed, "Now there's a road I've never been on!"

At a right angle from Old Pound Road, an unpaved sandy road, no more than two car lengths wide, went past one side of the pound and through the trees for several hundred yards before disappearing down a gradual slope. Not far from where we were standing was a rusting metal post, its four feet or so tilting slightly away from the road, clasping a once-white street sign with faded blue letters that read Blueberry Lane. Leaning against the post was a metallic sign, nearly as tall, with an arrow pointing down the shaded road and beneath it, in bright orange, were the words *For Sale*. Judging by the condition of the sign, it had not been exposed to the New Hampshire elements for many days.

"What could possibly be for sale down there?" Bette wondered aloud. "Let's go find out."

She hesitated, probably expecting me to check my wristwatch one more time, but I fooled her. "Let's do it!"

My camcorder was aimed out the front window as Bette drove carefully through what seemed like a huge green tunnel of foliage while occasional squirrels and red chipmunks dashed madly in front of us. The towering pines and white birches from one side of the road reached across to brush gently against their neighbors on the other and my words

17

are forever preserved on tape. "Look at this! It's almost as if we're riding into another world . . . some sort of enchanted woodland in a Disney movie!"

Suddenly we emerged into bright sunshine at the bottom of a gentle incline. Beyond the stone wall to our right was a meadow of thick grass sprinkled with Shasta daisies, black-eyed Susans, sunflowers, and an occasional red poppy for perhaps fifty yards parallel with the road. . . . And then we both saw it at the same time . . . an old white farmhouse standing proudly, serenely, and very much alone. No neighbors. Not even another house in sight. And close to the road, at the end of an old red-brick stone walk, stood another *For Sale* sign with name and phone number.

Bette turned into the vacant yard to the left of the house, shut off the ignition, and looked at me. We said nothing. She opened her door and I opened mine and we walked, almost on tiptoe, across the front lawn heavy with clover up to the front door and knocked. No response. After several minutes we went around to a side door and knocked again. No answer.

"Look, Og," Bette sighed as she shaded her eyes with her hands and peered through a dusty window. "This is the kitchen. Can you see those huge ceiling beams . . . and the floor, with those wide pine boards? Wow! This may be an old-timer, but it has had a lot of love!"

"Hi, folks! It's a great old place, isn't it?"

Neither of us had heard his car drive up, but his smile was warm as he extended his hand to both of us. "My name is Bob Watterson. I live up the road there and just happened to be driving to my office. Saw your car and thought I might as well stop in case you have any questions. I sell a little real estate now and then, besides being a builder, and we just listed this house yesterday."

He was very familiar with the property, Bob explained, since he and his family had lived in it for several years before building a new home at his present location up the hill and around the corner. He said that the farm's most recent owner, a retired sea captain, had just decided a few weeks ago that he wanted a place closer to the ocean.

We told him that we felt a little foolish, because we had just been driving around doing a little sightseeing and that we regretted taking up his time, since we really were not looking for a house—we already had a lovely home in Scottsdale, Arizona. He shrugged his shoulders and kept smiling. Bette said, "If you had come by five minutes later we would have missed each other."

"Well," he shrugged again, still smiling, "maybe this was all meant to be. Do you have a little time? If you'd like to go inside and look around I'd be more than happy to show it to you."

And show it to us he did . . . all nine rooms and their features . . . the long, oak-paneled living room, which Bob said was part of the original 1870 structure . . . sun streaming through southern-exposure windows and glistening off wide planked-pine floors with old countersunk nail holes . . . the massive floor-to-ceiling fireplace . . . coins, dated in the last century, embedded at eye level in the dining room wall by some sentimental plasterer of old . . . oak beams stretching across the kitchen ceiling beneath a cathedral roof with skylight . . . an unfinished "summer room," off the kitchen, where friends probably sat and visited with a pitcher of lemonade during muggy July and August evenings . . . a rolling lawn of sorts behind the house, studded with huge boulders and bordered by azaleas and tall blueberry bushes, with an open woodland of pine and birch and oak and maple, all part of the four acres of property, we were told, slumbering beyond. As we stood in the backyard near the woods, the only sounds we could hear were the constant chirping from scores of birds obviously not too happy at our presence, a faraway train whistle, and the constant rustling in the breeze of long, elliptically shaped, dark green leaves that almost completely blanketed a stately white ash, nearly ninety feet tall, according to Bob, whose massive limbs extended protectively over the entire house.

Finally, Bette leaned close to me when Bob was out of earshot and gasped, "Hon, this place is talking to me!"

I nodded. "It's talking to me, too!"

Five hours later we wrote out a check covering the deposit on the farm.

Late in August we returned to New Hampshire for the closing.

Very often, playing chess with God can be an unforgettable experience. . . .

III

In my speeches I am frequently reminding audiences that all of us are passengers on this shrinking spaceship called Earth . . . a fragile vehicle constantly spinning at a speed of more than one thousand miles per hour at its equator while circling the sun at a mind-boggling speed of more than sixty-six thousand miles per hour!

Actually, we are not passengers but prisoners on this hurtling ball of rock and vegetation and water, shackled to its surface by gravitational forces along with billions of others, all with the same innate goal . . . survival.

For countless centuries we have struggled against the forces of our environment . . . enemies bent on our destruction or, at the very least, our slavery. We have overcome glaciers, drought, floods, fire, and famine and emerged from each adversity as better human beings. We have not, unfortunately, fared so well when it comes to the terrible trauma of pulling up our roots and turning our back on familiar places and friendly faces in order to continue our life in a different environment, for a multiplicity of reasons, among strangers.

Several weeks after we returned to Arizona and the shock of our actions in New Hampshire had somewhat subsided, Bette and I worked out what we believed was a perfect solution to this unexpected and unnecessary crisis we had created in our lives. We would keep both homes and make the Langville farm our summer place, thus escaping the seemingly unending string of 100–plus degree days that always transforms the southern half of Arizona into an unbearable inferno from May to September. That way we'd have the best of both worlds . . . spring and summer in New Hampshire's lush green Monadnock region and fall and winter in Arizona's famed Valley of the Sun.

In early November we were back in Langville, this time accompanied by our oldest son, Dana, a lover of Early American homes who has a lot of architectural savvy. Dana spent several days going through the old place with pad and pencil in hand and finally reviewed with us, very carefully, what he believed needed to be done in order to make our old house functional and comfortable. Top priority, Dana believed, was converting the unfinished and obviously neglected summer room into a writing studio for me . . . with insulation, carpeting, plenty of built-in floor-to-ceiling bookshelves, new windows, wallpaper, and a gas fireplace. If we then decided to spend entire summers in Langville I would be able to work in as much comfort as I enjoyed in our Scottsdale home. Dana also had many other suggestions such as rebuilding one of the bathrooms, replacing the battered stairway to the second floor, extending the small upstairs master bedroom an additional twenty-five feet to include a large closet and converting the extended room beneath it into an entertainment center to hold a projection television unit and stereo system. In all, his list of suggestions filled two legal-sized pages, and we bought all of them. We then had a meeting with Bob Watterson and after he gave us his estimate for the entire remodeling job we contracted with him to do it all. Since the holidays were fast approaching, the three of us returned to Arizona with Bob's assurances that all the renovation and additions would certainly be completed by the following June in time for us to fully enjoy summer in New Hampshire.

Our plans changed, suddenly and dramatically, one morning early in December as we were driving to Phoenix from our Scottsdale home to do some additional Christmas shopping for our grandchildren. Moving along Lincoln Drive, with the lovely city's skyline below us and to our left, we both shook our heads in helpless frustration at the ugly dark cloud of pollution that hovered threateningly over the downtown area, a sight that was becoming so common that most of us were beginning to take it for granted. As we drew closer to the tall office buildings and downtown malls, we began to creep along in traffic so congested that it was close to being complete gridlock. Soon the inside of our automobile began to reek of foul-smelling fumes from exhaust pipes, and Bette began coughing. After finally catching her breath, she turned to me with watery eyes and rasped, "Og, let's get out of here!"

"Hey, we're already downtown. Let's do what we came to do, first. . . ."

"No, no, hon. . . . I don't mean let's get out of

this mess right now. I mean let's sell the Scottsdale house and go live on our old farm all year!"

"Do you know what you're saying? Right now
there's more than two feet of snow on the ground
back there, according to Bob. How will you feel
when you won't be able to get your car out of the
garage for three or four days?"

"I'll love it. I'd be able to get to some of those
sewing and knitting projects I keep putting
aside—and just think how much more writing you
could do if there was no temptation, each day, to
run to the country club for another round of golf.
We'd both be more productive . . . and probably
live a lot longer, too, if we weren't inhaling all this
garbage. And there are ways of handling that
snow back there. I've always wanted a Jeep Grand
Wagoneer. . . ."

Soon after Christmas, we listed our Scottsdale home with the same realtor, Marby Pruitt,
who had sold us the property when it was new,
fifteen years earlier. Marby had remained our
good friend through the years. In a very "down"
real estate market, she demonstrated why she
was one of the best in the state by selling our
place in exactly six months.

Shortly after the sale, I was chatting on the
phone with an old friend, Jim Newman, one of the
few authentic geniuses I have ever known and
founder of The PACE Organization, a company
conducting powerful seminars that help people
release their untapped potential. Jim's lovely
wife, Nan, whom Bette and I both treasure as a
friend, had joined us on their extension line as
always but instead of her usually bright remarks

she was just gasping in dismay as I told Jim the entire story of how we had accidentally found the old farmhouse and were about to make some radical changes in our life-style. Finally I said, "Jim, I really don't understand any of it. We had it made here . . . every luxury and comfort imaginable . . . not much mortgage remaining. . . . I really cannot believe we are doing this!"

I could hear Jim chuckling. "I know why it's happening, Og. You were becoming too complacent. Things were getting too easy for you. You had run out of challenges. Best-selling author . . . Hall of Fame speaker . . . you needed to be challenged again . . . to be resurrected from that calm, easy routine of yours. This is really the best thing in the world that could have happened to you and Bette."

And so, approximately seventeen months after Bette and I had first visited Langville's historic old animal pound and then allowed our curiosity to lead us down a dirt road, a United Van Lines tractor and trailer, after a 2,580-mile cross-country haul on eighteen fat tires, inched carefully and very slowly down Blueberry Lane, its huge wheels completely straddling the narrow roadway. During the next two days, more than 24,500 pounds of furniture and all our other worldly possessions, packed carefully (we hoped) in cartons of many sizes, were unloaded from the cavernous depths of the huge van by a crew of four and piled, often ceiling-high, throughout every old, creaking room of our adopted country homestead.

Exhausted, hurting, hungry, and sleepy, Bette and I stood in the center of Blueberry Lane and watched as the red taillights of the van finally disappeared behind a screen of trees after turning right onto Old Pound Road. The stars overhead seemed low enough to touch, while a nearly full moon cast a soft glow over our farm and the silent surrounding woods. Bette moved closer to me and we hugged for several minutes before she pushed me back and said in a hoarse voice, "Go ahead, wise guy, say it!"

"Say what?"

"I've been waiting all day for you to give me the business . . . for you to exclaim in your very best speech-delivery tones . . ."

"Exclaim what? What are you talking about?"

"Og, I've been waiting to hear you say . . . 'Just think, Bette, no more endless Scottsdale shopping malls for you to waste your time and money in, no more sitting around our pool with a good book, no more golf every other day, no more Bermuda shorts in January, no more pink grapefruit and navel oranges to pick in our backyard, no more year-long tan, no more authentic Mexican food for us to stuff ourselves on, no more freshly picked roses from our garden for the Christmas table . . . but . . . but . . . it was all worth it, Bette. See! Take a deep breath! Wow! No pollution!'"

She was giggling. Very proud of her performance.

I didn't know whether to laugh . . . or cry.

IV

It was a day I shall never forget.

We had survived our first Langville winter despite a record-breaking frigid December and, at last, all traces of snow had finally vanished and the grounds were no longer muddy. I had spent some of the morning slowly walking our property to determine how much cutting and clearing and grading and landscaping would be required to make the outside as inviting and comfortable as Bob Watterson and Curt and Edd and Sam and Cam and Jerry and Bruce had made the inside of our home with all of their alterations, renovations, additions, electrical work, plumbing changes, painting, and wallpapering, not to mention the authentic period furniture and decorating expertise supplied us by a unique Concord store called Country Primitive and its talented owner, Andrew Biancur.

A stubborn April fog still lingered below the treetops in the damp woodlands behind our farm although it was now getting close to noon. For the past hour or so I had been cutting back thick and thorny masses of rosebushes that lay sprawling and neglected throughout the yard. Hopefully, among the many stalks I pruned, there might be a few rare varieties of those beloved, old-fashioned,

27

sweet-smelling damask, Bourbon, or hybrid perpetual roses of the last century that may have blossomed in exquisite colors back when our farmhouse was new.

The more Bette and I had studied our four-plus acres of New Hampshire farmland, the more we became convinced that we should retain the natural look of the area wherever possible and stay away completely from any sort of formal landscaping. If dandelions happened to flourish in various sections of the undulating and rocky lawn we would let them be . . . not to mention violets, bluets, and occasional clumps of lilies of the valley. When I finally did complete the trimming back of shrubs, trees, roses, and berry bushes to some sort of respectable shape, the yard work, from then on, would consist of little more than mowing what Bette called her "unsophisticated" lawn. We were both determined not ever to become slaves to the old homestead we had already grown to love so much during our first six months of residence.

I finally lowered myself wearily onto a large, flat, granite boulder near the woods and placed my old portable General Electric radio by my side on the stone. The tough old AM receiver, nearly the size of a lunch box and a gift back in 1965, had been my constant companion for the past quarter century in all the yard work I had performed around our Illinois and Arizona homes. Through the years it had been dropped, kicked, stepped on, and left out in the rain countless times, yet it still sounded rich and powerful. Now it was tuned to a Boston radio station, WBZ, whose strong signal came in loud and clear from eighty miles to the south. It had been my mother's favorite when I was growing up just twenty miles from Boston in the small town of Natick, back in the thirties, and so my old beat-up music and chatter box was now permanently tuned to that station. Somehow it made me feel closer to the lady who had been so important in my life.

I had just spent the better part of January and February touring the country to promote my new book, *A Better Way to Live*, for Bantam Books and in so many interviews from coast to coast, on radio, television, and with the press, I had been asked again and again about that special chapter in the new book that had described my mother's dream for her kid . . . that someday I would be "a writer . . . not just a writer but a great writer!" My tough little Irish mother died only a few weeks after I graduated from Natick High in 1940 and for many terrible years it appeared that her dream for me was a lost cause until, in my early forties, I wrote a small book called *The Greatest Salesman in the World* and my entire life changed. Although all the details were in the new book, many radio and television hosts still insisted on hearing me personally relate the story of my rise from a derelict to a best-selling author, including that fateful day in my life when I flew to New York City and was told by Bantam Book executives that they had purchased the paperback rights to *The Greatest Salesman in the World* for more money than I believed was in the U.S. Treasury. Rushing from Bantam's headquarters on Fifth Avenue back to my hotel, the New York Hilton, to phone Bette with the good news, I was trapped in a horrendous thunderstorm and with no raincoat to protect me I dashed into an open church doorway. I can still remember hearing the rain pounding on the roof and an organ, or a tape recording of an organ, playing "Amazing Grace" in the basement as I walked slowly up to the front of the empty church, fell to my knees, and sobbed, half-aloud, "Mom, wherever you are, I want you to know we finally made it!"

And now, after all my years of wandering, all my years of failure and success, here I was in a pair of old blue jeans still doing chores in a small-town backyard as I had done in my youth, with a backdrop of pines and birches so similar to that old Natick home, only a two-hour drive . . . and fifty years away. I had come full circle, and what a circle it had been . . . from the poorest kid on the school bus, with immigrant parents . . . to the International Speakers Hall of Fame plus millions of books sold in eighteen languages. At that very moment I could almost feel my mother's presence and hear her voice saying, "Welcome home!"

Minutes later I felt even closer to my mother and the past. My old, beat-up radio was demanding my attention! With a cheering crowd and police sirens as a background, an excited male voice was talking about the marathon and this year's record number of runners, including several previous winners plus Italy's 1988 Olympic marathon champion.

"My God!" I heard myself saying. "This must be Patriots' Day down in Massachusetts. They're running the BAA Marathon today! Now I know I've come home!"

Patriots' Day. A legal holiday in the Bay State. Why? It came back to me quickly. Minutemen! The Old North Church! "One, if by land, or two, if by sea" . . . or was it water? There had been Paul Revere's midnight ride to warn his neighbors that the British were coming and . . . our first victory at Concord, when embattled farmers drove the British soldiers all the way back to Boston after firing the shot heard 'round the world on Lexington Common.

For reasons I never understood as a kid, or questioned, the annual Patriots' Day marathon from Hopkinton to Boston was always a special event in our family. Since there was no cost to watch this annual spectacle, that may have explained its popularity in our house, because there was little money to spend on entertainment of any sort. In any event, each year my mother and father and I, and later my baby sister, would travel in our Model-T Ford to Dennison Crossing, Framingham, only a mile from our house, park the car right on Waverly Street, the actual race route, and, clutching our *Daily Record* with all the runners' numbers listed on the tabloid's back page, we would loudly cheer and applaud and encourage the participants as they passed our vantage point, commencing at approximately thirty minutes after the starter's gun was fired at high noon in Hopkinton and lasting until the final struggling soul, followed by ambulances and press cars, went past an hour or so later.

As I sat engulfed in memories, listening to the

announcer bravely struggling to pronounce some
of the names of African runners who were in the
leading cluster of marathoners, another runner's
name suddenly came to me from the long ago
past . . . Johnny Kelley. I tried but couldn't remember the exact year when my mother had
adopted him as her favorite because—why else?
—he was Irish. I can still recall, vividly, that
special race moment when Johnny Kelley ran by,
close to the leaders. My mother, completely out of
character, leaned close to Kelley as he passed and
yelled, "God bless you, Johnny Kelley! Win one for
the Irish, please!" Well, he did win, and I can still
see the front-page newspaper photo of his smiling
face, with arms raised high, as he broke the
victory tape in Boston. What year was that? How
old was I? No clues. As I sat on the stone and
listened to my old radio, I couldn't remember.

And then, something I heard nearly lifted me
off the rock. I seized my abused portable and drew
it close to my face. The announcer was talking
about Johnny Kelley. What was he saying? Yes,
that's it! That was the year! 1935! The radio voice
had just said that Johnny Kelley the Elder . . . to
differentiate him from another marathoner named
Johnny Kelley of later years . . . had won his
first marathon in 1935! Quick calculation! I had
been just eleven years old when my mother, with
my all-out assistance, had cheered Johnny Kelley
on to victory while my father watched us and
smiled patiently. But why was the sportscaster
talking about Kelley now . . . fifty-five years
later? What? What did he say? Dear God, did I
hear correctly? Yes . . . yes, I did! The voice was

saying that Kelley was running as smoothly as ever and waving and smiling at the crowd. Johnny Kelley? Our Johnny Kelley? Can't be. It's a common name. There are thousands of Irishmen named Johnny Kelley in Massachusetts. But no . . . it was not just any Johnny Kelley! It was *our* Johnny Kelley . . . *my mother's and mine!* He was now passing the Framingham-Natick line on West Central Street. Johnny Kelley! Our Kelley! The announcer's voice was tinged with admiration and awe. Johnny Kelley was running in his fifty-ninth BAA Marathon and looking good! Johnny Kelley, age 83, the man whom Mom and I had cheered ourselves hoarse over in 1935, was *still* running over those same old streets heading for that distant finish line, almost twenty miles away, in Boston. "God bless you, Johnny Kelley!" I buried my face in my hands. I was sobbing. Then I turned off the radio and rose.

I walked across the rear deck and entered the house through glass dining room doors, placing my radio on the hand-planed cherry sideboard before continuing on through to the front hallway. Except for the grandfather clock, our home was very still. Bette was shopping in Manchester. I opened the front door and stepped out into the sunlight again, inhaling the freshness of approaching spring. I was puzzled. What was happening to me? Why was I reliving so much of my past, lately, when I never had before? Authors especially, I guess, were supposed to be extremely grateful if they were blessed with the kind of memory that enabled them to draw on their earlier life experiences, but whenever I was writing and needed to recall some specific incident in my past it had always been a terrible struggle to revive the facts. Not any more. Since moving to Langville, events and people from bygone years kept popping from my memory bank with no effort, like that Johnny Kelley matter. Perhaps Langville and the return to New England was the catalyst. Maybe living again in the same climate and so close to my childhood roots was the trigger. I shook my head. A good walk might clear the cobwebs from my mind and free me from the shadows and memories of other years with all their tears and their laughter. I wasn't ready to write my memoirs yet!

My heavy yard shoes made loud and rhythmic crunching sounds on the dirt as I trudged slowly along Blueberry Lane. Spring was tiptoeing its way into New Hampshire. Tiny curling fern fronds were beginning to appear on both sides of the road, and the maple trees were already budding. What a lucky man I was! What a wonderful place to live, for all seasons, with the lady I loved. I hoped we would never move again.

When I was perhaps a hundred yards from the house, heading toward Old Pound Road, I heard a branch snap in the underbrush to my right and I stopped dead in my tracks, just in time to see a tiny red fox stroll leisurely out onto the road. He was less than twenty feet away and staring directly at me, but his instincts must have assured him that I was harmless because he didn't quicken pace at all, finally disappearing over the stone wall to my left.

Hands buried deep in my jacket pockets, a

habit from my youth, I continued walking. A penetrating, throbbing hum from a single-engine plane circling above was the perfect counterpoint to the hushed woods on both sides of Blueberry Lane. When I arrived at the corner I turned until I was once again face to face with the old pound, that animal refuge from another century that Bette had insisted on showing me during that fateful afternoon, two years before, when we should have been on the way to Boston. Since our arrival, whenever I had driven by that old and unique construction, I always thought about stopping and spending enough time to become truly familiar with the ancient landmark. That hour was finally at hand.

I moved carefully down the steep incline from the road and approached the rear wall of stones where there was an opening approximately four feet wide. This space, I remembered Bette telling me, was where the lost animals were led inside before stones, or perhaps logs, were rolled against the opening so that the livestock would not escape until their owners eventually retrieved them. I walked through the opening and stepped down, perhaps two feet. Now I could barely see Blueberry Lane and Old Pound Road above the uneven tiers of boulders that had been fitted so perfectly atop each other that there was little or no daylight between any of them. The floor of the pound was soft with fallen leaves and overgrown with weeds, ferns, and some tiny wild berry bushes. In one corner was a cluster of four birch trees, each rising at least sixty feet between several tall pines. I wondered about the birches. Had they begun their growth only after the pound was no longer used as an animal haven, or had they survived their early years despite the constant traffic of sheep and goats and cows?

I stood motionless and listened. From the underbrush, deeper in the woods, there were soft crackling sounds. Tiny feet scampering over dry leaves and branches. Overhead, a strange and almost-moaning birdcall echoed through the trees. I leaned back and rubbed my hands against the soft velvet-like moss that covered the boulders, trying to imagine this very special place serving the community, on a morning like this, during the beginning years of the nineteenth century! 1817? A long time ago. I remembered one day, when I was unpacking my many cartons of books in my new studio, formerly the old farm's summer room, I had come across a favorite source-book of mine, entitled *The Timetables of History*. Recalling the year that the pound had been erected, according to its bronze plaque, I had paused in my unpacking, flopped on the new carpet, and turned to the year 1817. What was going on in the world while Langville's small village of farmers was erecting its pound? I needed a yardstick of some sort to help me measure the passage of time so that I could better appreciate the historical landmark in my own neighborhood. Well, in 1817, James Monroe had been inaugurated our nation's fifth president. Mississippi became our twentieth state. Construction commenced on the Erie Canal, Waterloo Bridge opened in London, and Baltimore became the first city in the United States to have its streets illuminated by gaslights. And on July twelfth of that year, an impoverished young man and his wife, John and Cynthia Thoreau, became the proud parents of Henry David.

The air in the pound had suddenly become eerily still, and a wonderful feeling of gratitude as well as tranquility settled over me. How very special it was to be alive at that very moment! I looked around the pound in awe. No outdoor place of worship, I thought, could ever be as peaceful or closer to God than this old arrangement of stones seemed to be at that very moment.

"Mister Og, you are looking wonderful!"

Instinctively I held my breath. There had been no sound of an automobile on either Old Pound Road or Blueberry Lane, nor had I heard any footsteps approaching the pound from any direction, and yet I had just heard a male voice, slightly hoarse but still a rich basso profundo, speaking so close to me that I knew he had to be within the pound or just outside the wall. I remained almost absolutely still, trying to collect my thoughts. I had just walked around the entire inside of the small pound and could swear that no one was within the enclosure except me! After a few dozen combat missions over Germany, in my youth, I had never frightened very easily but now I could feel my old heart thumping as I slowly turned only my head toward the direction of the voice.

Leaning against the inside of the south wall, no more than ten steps away, was an old man who was nodding and smiling at me. Although he was bald across the top of his brown scalp, thick gray hair grew above both ears and flowed loosely down behind his neck. His full beard was almost white beneath a straight and prominent nose, high cheekbones, and a face that belonged in an old masters painting with hundreds of deeply etched wrinkles. He was dressed in a faded brown corduroy jacket, blue jeans, and brown boots. Around his neck was a red woolen scarf and in his mouth was a corncob pipe, unlit. He raised both arms in a friendly gesture of welcome as he continued to smile, and I finally took several steps toward him before coming to an abrupt halt. The old man had moved away from the wall, and now that he was standing upright I could see that he towered well above my six feet. He smiled again, beckoning me to come closer with his huge hands as if I were a timid child. I inhaled deeply and hardly recognized my voice when I said, "Who are you? Your voice sounds familiar. You look familiar and yet I . . . and yet I . . ."

His deep laugh resounded through the woods and he leaned back against the rocks again, placing his left hand on the wall and extending the other toward me, waving it gently back and forward in his direction. "Come a little closer, Mister Og. You are certain to recognize an old friend if you do."

Mister Og? In the years since *The Greatest Miracle in the World* had first been published, in 1975, many had addressed me that way in person or in letters after reading the book, but no one had ever said it with as much love and respect as . . . as . . .

I ran the last few steps between us and we embraced. Both of us were sobbing. Finally I held him at arm's length and noticed, for the first time, beneath his scarf, the wooden cross attached to a thin leather cord that hung from his neck just as it had the first time I ever saw him, in Chicago, so many years ago.

"It is you! Dear God! Simon, Simon, Simon . . . !"

"It is, Mister Og, it is."

"Simon. Simon Potter. Oh, how I've missed you . . . and for so long!"

"And I have missed you, Mister Og . . . just as much . . . and just as long!"

V

"Now," I said softly, "let me get a good look at you."

After several minutes of silent embracing, I had taken the old man's hand and led him toward a portion of the pound's wall, running parallel to Blueberry Lane, that stood only two boulders high. What had been the third and top tier of stones from that section lay on the ground inside the pound, half-buried in decaying oak and maple leaves, probably dislodged from their original position by men or boys with little else to do.

Now Simon sat facing me on the low wall, our feet resting on the fallen boulders. I reached out, gently caressed his wrinkled cheeks, and shook my head in wonder. "Amazing! It's been—how long?—fifteen years since I last saw you and except for . . . forgive me . . . except for a little less hair on top, you haven't changed at all. Your birthday . . . the one that we celebrated in Chicago . . . help me . . . which one was that?"

He smiled and those warm, brown eyes opened wider. "You mean on that very special occasion when you and I planted your gift of a glass geranium outside in the cold in my second-story window box?"

"That's the one."

"The year was 1974 and that was my seventy-ninth birthday."

"My God, that means you are now . . . ninety-five years old! Look at you! What a miracle you are! Your eyes are clear, you stand just as tall and proud as back then, you felt as strong as an ironworker when you hugged me, and that beautiful voice still sounds like it should be performing at the Metropolitan Opera. What's your secret?"

"We are all surviving longer than our parents and grandparents, Mister Og. In 1900 only one in twenty-five lived to celebrate his or her sixty-fifth birthday. Today one in eight in this country is beyond that age. A child born back around the turn of the century could expect to live, on average, only forty years. Today's babies, with any luck at all, will make it to seventy-five. America is indeed turning gray. Already we 'over sixty-fivers' outnumber our teenagers. You want my secret for my long, long life? There is no secret. My reaching this very advanced age, so many years beyond even today's improved death rate, seems to be some sort of mysterious bonus granted to nearly all of God's ragpickers . . . to just about every individual who willingly renders aid and comfort and caring to those less fortunate. Now this great benefit for acting as one's brother's or sister's keeper, in volunteer work without pay, may still be a secret but I can assure you it will not remain so very long. Many reputable journals, such as *Psychology Today, Longevity,* and even my old favorite, *Better Homes and Gardens,* are already calling the public's attention to this mysterious connection between being what I would call a ragpicker . . . a giver of oneself, if you will . . . and additional years of life."

Simon Potter reading *Better Homes and Gardens?* That was a picture difficult to imagine until I reminded myself that the old man's quest for truth had always been unlimited in its range and passion. He leaned forward, his elbows resting on his knees while he studied his folded hands. "Mister Og, as you know, my profession, my avocation, my hobby, my life's mission for several decades has been that of a ragpicker. However, unlike other ragpickers, I salvage not empty beer and pop containers and old newspapers and cast-off clothes, but people . . . individuals who have fallen on bad times and find themselves, at last, on life's rubbish heaps. With much patience and work and the help of God I have been truly fortunate to rescue many lives and thus provide them with another chance to fulfill their true destinies, including many who have nearly drowned in the terrible whirlpool of alcohol and drugs, two deadly enemies that are now penetrating every level of our society."

The old man patted my knee. "I believe I have even been able to make some contributions to your life. You are a much better man today, Mister Og, than you were back in the mid-seventies when we would meet and chat in my small apartment in Chicago, near your office, after you had spent long and difficult days as president of W. Clement Stone's excellent magazine, *Success Unlimited.* Your many books and your countless speeches on success, around the world, have contributed much to humanity since you resigned your position, in 1976, to devote, as you said, all your time to writing, lecturing . . . and golfing."

"You know what I've been doing?"

He nodded. "I have been following your activities closely. But first, let me finish with this longevity matter, because it is so very important and with your great following, perhaps you might choose to spread the word. First, there are four very simple rules that one must live by in order to increase the odds of a longer life and everyone knows what they are although I'm afraid that many lack the necessary fortitude or pride in themselves to observe them. First, just use some common sense in the amounts and types of food you stuff into yourself. You need no calorie or nutritional expert standing by to guide you. Second rule . . . when it comes to drugs and alcohol turn away, completely, except for perhaps an occasional glass of wine on a special occasion. Third," he said, wincing as he held up his battered and unlit corncob pipe, "put nothing in your mouth that is smoking at its other end. The fourth rule is to exercise moderately, at least three times a week. A thirty-minute brisk walk will do just fine. Jogging so many miles each day that you are in excruciating pain and ready to drop is not required. Just be certain you remain active and never, never fall slave to that television set. Those who are referred to as 'couch potatoes' are committing the most insidious and saddest form of suicide known to this generation."

Simon then raised both his hands, fingers extended like some great maestro, to emphasize what he was about to say. "Now, my dear friend, any child over the age of ten could have probably given you those four commonsense steps to a longer life, but the fifth and most important step is little known as yet, although its value is so great that it can multiply, perhaps by a factor of two or three, those additional years anyone can add to their life by following the first four rules. Are you ready . . . ?"

It was like old times. The master was teaching. The pupil was learning. "I'm ready!"

"Practice altruism!"

"Altruism?"

Simon seemed to be enjoying the puzzled look on my face. "Altruism, Mister Og, according to Webster's, is an unselfish regard for, or devotion to, the welfare of others. For reasons that science and medicine do not even understand as yet, it appears that those who give of their time and energy to assist others, on a volunteer basis and with no expected reward, seem to suffer from far less stress and depression in their lives while enjoying many more invigorating moments of self-satisfaction, pride, and a greater capacity for work, along with peace and contentment. Also, anyone fueled by these positive life charges will rarely suffer through the negative jolts of self-pity, hopelessness, and failure that always cause so much damage to anyone's immune system. What is so amazing is that several of the bright minds currently researching this whole area of longevity have come to believe that while we are in the process of helping others unselfishly, our body seems to release pain-relieving chemicals called endorphins, which athletes identify as the element that produces a runner's high."

"What a great recruiting tool for those organizations seeking volunteers, such as the American Red Cross, United Way, and Big Brothers. Join us and live longer!"

Simon scowled at what he probably mistook as my levity. "Mister Og, this is not some crackpot speculation that you might find in your newsstand scandal sheets. As down-to-earth a magazine as *Better Homes and Gardens* conducted a survey of its readers, asking how they felt when they regularly helped others voluntarily. The responses, turned over to the Institute for the Advancement of Health for analysis and review, indicated that a large percentage of those who assisted others through volunteer work actually became aware of a warm and pleasant physical sensation that has come to be referred to as a 'helper's high.' So you see, sir, less food and alcohol, no smoking, a little more exercise, and a lot of practiced altruism, perhaps in your own neighborhood, will contribute greatly toward your chances of hanging around long enough to see your grandchildren grow up. And that, my old friend, probably explains why you think I look so good for my advanced years. I'm a ragpicker, and all ragpickers practice a lot of altruism every day. Anyone can join our club. No dues. No meetings. And financial contributions to worthy causes, I might add, do not seem to have any effect on one's longevity. You've got to give of yourself and your time with no thought of any reward of any kind . . . not even a 'thank you.'"

"Albert Schweitzer?"

The old man's face lit up. "A perfect example. Writer, musician, theologian, philosopher . . . one of the world's all-time men of talent and wisdom, and yet for the last fifty years of his life, as a medical missionary, he ran a hospital in the jungle with his own funds for the natives of French Equatorial Africa . . . a hospital he literally built with his own hands. They buried him at ninety."

"Simon, I remember reading somewhere that he was in great condition, both mentally and physically, almost to the very end, and he once said that the only thing that made him feel old was all the mail he received that he was unable to answer."

"And how about you, Mister Og, are you still personally answering all your mail as you were doing when I first met you?"

I could feel my heart pounding just a little faster. His question had given me that perfect opening that I had been silently praying would eventually come. I hoped the wise old man would detect no trembling in my voice when I replied, "I try very hard and although there are many days when that overflowing 'In' basket makes me feel as old as Schweitzer, I do reply to every letter. Now and then, of course, I receive correspondence I am unable to answer because the sender has not included a return address. One such letter, way back in December of 1974, is still as vivid in my mind as if it had arrived yesterday. I had come into work at the magazine very early on a Monday morning in order to begin catching up on two weeks' work because I had been touring the country to promote a new book. On my desk was a manila envelope, addressed to me but with the stamps in the upper right-hand corner still uncanceled. The package contained a farewell letter from you, Simon, also a safety pin holding a small piece of white rag which your letter referred to as a 'ragpicker's amulet' plus the special gift you had been promising me for several months, 'The God Memorandum,' containing the four secrets of success and happiness. In your letter you asked me to wear the amulet and practice the rules for success and happiness in my own life for a hundred days and if they worked for me I was then free to share them with the world. There was absolutely no indication as to why you had vanished with no warning or where you had gone. Losing you was almost as terrible a shock to me as my mother's sudden death when I was sixteen."

The old man was leaning forward, staring only at his hands. I touched his shoulder softly but he didn't look up. "Simon," I said, "I couldn't respond to your letter. No return address. And when I raced to your apartment, across from the parking lot behind our building . . . when I went up the stairs to that familiar and peaceful place where we had spent so many precious moments together, I discovered that no one knew you at all and there was a strange family living in your apartment who had never heard of you or couldn't even recognize you from my description. I even checked with the police and the morgue. No Simon Potter. Not a clue. It was a terrible time for me, and just about my only solace was a sentence in your letter that mentioned that we would not see each other for a long time. I was grasping at straws but at least I took that to mean that someday, someday . . . we might be together again. A bullet in my stomach would have been less painful than your mysterious departure without any explanation or farewell. I had grown to love you so much and all your wise advice had given me a valuable and balanced perspective on life that has guided me for many years."

Simon finally raised his head, sighed, and stared down Blueberry Lane. "You wrote about all of this, Mister Og, in your book, *The Greatest Miracle in the World.*"

"I certainly did, and I included 'The God Memorandum' as you had suggested in the letter, because it had truly been of great benefit to me. And even the book had a mysterious disappearance connected with it. Another loss to me. When I write a book I always keep all my notes in file folders, usually by book chapters, so that I can quickly refer to any portion of them later if need be. Well, just before the book was published I went looking for the file containing the original copy from you of 'The God Memorandum,' which I had placed in a folder marked 'Chapter Nine.' I had decided that the 'Memorandum' should be placed in my safe-deposit box rather than kept in a file cabinet and that if I ever went on tour to promote *The Greatest Miracle in the World* it would be nice to have the original document with me to show the world. That folder was not in the cabinet with the others, and I have never been able to locate it. I didn't know what to think. I still don't."

Simon continued to stare down Blueberry

Lane. "But Mister Og," he said without moving his head, "when Bantam Books purchased the paperback rights in 1977 and then sent you on a lengthy tour to promote the book, I know you were asked, again and again, whether any of the incidents in the book had ever happened to you and if there was really an old ragpicker named Simon Potter or it was all a figment of your imagination."

I grinned. "They're still asking me those same questions . . . after all these years."

Finally he turned, and his old eyes were moist. "And you have always responded, to all those who ask, in the very same manner, have you not?"

"I've never had much of a choice, Simon. No proof of your existence. No witnesses who ever saw you in the neighborhood or apartment building. No 'God Memorandum' to show anyone. And so, whenever I've been pressed as to whether any of that book was true or was Simon Potter just a figment of my imagination, I always tell the person asking to pick up a Bible and turn to John 4:48 . . . and then I tell them that is the only answer I ever give."

"I know." Simon closed his eyes and spoke softly. "*Then said Jesus unto him, except ye see signs and wonders, ye will not believe.*"

"That's it . . . and that's all. The book was aptly named. It was a great miracle and it has sold in the millions of copies. Even now, after all these years, it is still on Waldenbooks' Religion and Inspirational paperback bestseller list. And then, a year ago, I flew to New York City and spent two days at the RCA studios, with a cast of Broadway actors, recording the book as a ninety-minute drama that Bantam Books issued on cassette. I'm very proud of it. The one problem we had was finding an actor who sounded like you. I don't know how many we auditioned before Leslie Corn, the brilliant lady who heads up the production company assigned to produce our recording, finally worked her magic."

"Yes," he nodded, "Stephen Newman was an excellent choice. Marvelous diction and a fine actor."

I sat bolt upright and looked into his face. "You know . . . you even know the name of the person who played you in our recording at RCA?"

"I do."

"Would you like to explain to your old friend through what mysterious channels you have been able to keep up with my activities, apparently day by day and even minute by minute?"

"No."

"Well, let's try a different sort of question. After all the love and respect and wonderful moments we had together, as you taught me how to enjoy a life filled with success and happiness, why did you suddenly vanish without so much as a handshake?"

He lowered his head as a scolded child would do and his voice was only a whisper. "Mister Og, my beloved friend, I cannot tell you any more than this . . . an emergency situation had arisen, and apparently I was the only ragpicker with the knowledge and experience to deal with it."

That frightening statement opened up more possible questions than it answered, but I knew full well that I couldn't push this saintly man. He continued, "I had written my farewell letter and prepared the package for you with the amulet and 'God Memorandum' several weeks before it was delivered. I delayed walking out of your life as long as possible because I knew how much I would miss your warm companionship and those marvelous discussions, even though it was obvious that you didn't need me. . . . Anyone could see that your future would be blessed with much good."

"Not even a farewell hug, for God's sake?"

"No. Both of us would have suffered unnecessary pain. I anguished about my decision for several days before deciding that the best way was just to vanish and let time do the healing as it always does. Believe me, it was better that way for both of us."

"And was your emergency ragpicking project successful?"

"Very much so, I am proud to say. A famous musician. You would know his name. All is well."

A car was coming up Old Pound Road, the first I had heard since Simon and I had greeted each other. I turned and saw it was Bette. As her gold Jeep Grand Wagoneer turned left off Old Pound onto Blueberry Lane, I quickly swung both my legs over the stone wall and clambered up the banking to the street, yelling and waving my arms.

Bette hit the brakes as only she can do, rolled down her window, and shouted, "What's the matter? Are you okay?"

"I've never been better . . . and this is just about the best day of my life!"

I pulled open her front door and extended my hand. "Come on out! There's a very special person here that I want you to meet . . . and you'll never believe this!"

Bette stepped down from the Wagoneer's high front seat and glanced anxiously over my shoulder toward the pound. "Believe what?"

"Someone very special is here. I think it's a miracle."

I turned toward the place on the wall where Simon and I had sat through our entire conversation. No one was there. The old pound was vacant.

VI

Several hours passed before I could bring myself to talk about my strange experience at the old pound. Bette never came close to my studio during the afternoon, while I tried very hard to keep my mind off Simon by catching up with my mail, and during supper she did little more than ramble on about her frustrating morning search for casual summer outfits at Manchester's New Hampshire Mall. Not until after we had loaded up the dishwasher and I lay stretched out on our favorite living room couch did I finally tell her everything that had happened earlier that day, following my innocent stroll up Blueberry Lane.

As soon as I began talking, Bette stopped work on the afghan square she was knitting and listened intently, eyes half shut, not once interrupting or challenging any portion of my story. Although she had never met or even seen Simon Potter during those earlier days in Chicago when the old man and I had grown so close to each other, she was very familiar with just about every detail of the venerable ragpicker's chapter in my life. She, more than anyone else, realized how much Simon's wise advice and counsel had affected my future, making me a much better father and husband and human being than I had been before the old man's words touched my very soul.

When I finished narrating my story of our strange reunion at the pound, Bette remained silent for several moments before she frowned and said, "Hon, the mystery of Simon just seems to grow deeper with the years. There are so many questions I'd like to ask your old friend."

"Like what . . . ?"

"Well, during all those months you two were so close, back in Chicago, why is it that no one else knew him or ever saw him . . . except you? And now, why did he vanish again . . . just when you were about to introduce me to the great man at last?"

I remained silent. Bette leaned toward me, waving a knitting needle. "Want more?"

"Shoot!"

"Okay, how on earth did Simon manage to locate you, on this lonely dirt road, in the middle of nowhere . . . after all these years?"

"I don't know. He did say that he has been tracking my activities ever since his sudden departure more than fifteen years ago, but when I asked him to explain, he just passed on that one."

"I shouldn't wonder. Twenty-first-century radar? Sounds like an old episode of *The Twilight Zone*. Do you think you'll see him again?"

"God . . . I hope so."

Bette smiled. "Another book, maybe?"

"That never entered my mind. I just don't want to lose him again, and I'd love to hear his observations on what's going on in our world these days."

"Og, please, there is one question, above all

the others, that demands an answer, and my instincts tell me that how Simon answers it, if he does answer it, will go a long way toward foretelling your future . . . and, of course, mine too!"

"Now you've lost me."

"Just think about this. I assume that Simon is still functioning in this business of human salvage . . . rescuing humans in his unique role of ragpicker . . . after they have stumbled and fallen and suffered some sort of tragic failure or terrible loss in their lives."

"I'm sure he is. From all he said I gathered he was still active, and I seriously doubt that any ragpicker has a retirement age anyway. So long as there's any life in them at all, they just keep reaching out to others who need help. . . ."

"Then the big jackpot question you really should ask your special friend, if you meet again—and I think you will—is why is he here, in your life again, at this time. Why?"

On the following morning, after breakfast, I walked along Blueberry Lane to the old pound and sat on the lower wall again. I had invited Bette to join me but she just shook her head and replied, "He probably won't show if I'm along. You've got to do this solo."

Solo I sat in the shaded stillness for over an hour. Simon didn't show, and as I headed back to the farm a UPS delivery truck, in its familiar dark brown, went past me and I could see it turn into our driveway. The twenty-five pink Simplicity hedge roses I had ordered from Jackson and Perkins had arrived, to my great joy. Now I had something other than Simon to occupy my mind as well as aggravate my aging muscles. I immediately began the task—one that seemed to be getting more difficult each year I attempted it—of digging deep holes with my favorite pick and shovel. Those lovely roses had been selected to enhance a very special spot on two different levels of land separated by layers of granite boulders on the west side of the house.

On the following morning, before continuing with my rose planting, I took another brief stroll to the old pound, but I was back within the hour, mixing peat moss and dry cow manure to surround the plants' roots as I tucked them lovingly into the ground and watered them. Two days later, Bette and I flew to Chicago to join many of his friends and family in helping W. Clement Stone celebrate his eighty-eighth birthday. It was a special night for us, and I still don't understand what got into me, but as Bette and I were leaving I leaned over and kissed the great man on his cheek. Those years when I had edited his magazine, *Success Unlimited*, had actually been the turning point in my life.

When we returned from Chicago there was just about enough time for me to change suitcases and head for Nashville where I was scheduled to be the closing speaker on an all-star program sponsored by the Resource Group of America. I spent some quiet time at the pound, on the afternoon I returned, before catching another plane for St. Petersburg, and this time the speech was for the Small Business Council of that lovely city.

I slept late, following my weather-delayed return from St. Petersburg, but Bette finally came into the bedroom and said, "Hey, sleeping beauty, the UPS truck has made another visit and I think you've got more planting to do."

The garden work could wait. After my orange juice and scrambled eggs and coffee I first checked on the condition of my newly planted roses before walking up the road and sitting, once again, on the pound's boulders. Delicate green ferns on the floor of the pound had grown more than a foot in height and there were now so many of them that it was impossible to take a step anywhere inside the pound without crushing several fronds. How many trips had I now made to the old pound in vain? Was I really acting like a fool? Would he ever come?

The morning UPS delivery was several long cardboard packages containing a total of eighteen cultivated blueberry plants I had ordered from Miller Nurseries. First I pounded two stakes into the rocky ground on the north and south borders of our east meadow and ran heavy white twine from one stake to the other as a guide. Then I proceeded to test my old back to the limit by digging eighteen very wide and deep holes with my trusty tools, each hole spaced about five feet from the next, before carefully laying out the bushes in a specific planting order. Along with the proper mix of peat moss and aluminum sulphate, I placed them in the ground so that each year the first six plants in the row, named Ivanhoe and New Blueray, would produce berries first; the next six, Atlantic and Bluecrop, would bloom in mid-season; and the giant berries of Jersey and New Herbert would bloom perhaps two weeks later.

Og Mandino

Hopefully, fresh blueberry pies and muffins for two months or more! And how did I celebrate that final plant going into the ground? I walked the few hundred yards up to the corner and rested on my favorite boulder at the pound. Waiting. Waiting in vain. On the following morning I was on a plane again, this time heading for Sarasota, where I spoke to a warm and loving throng at the Van Wezel Performing Arts Hall.

Because of my nocturnal writing habits I have been a late riser for many years. Brunch in our house is a standard meal. However, only a few days after my return from Sarasota, I awoke at daybreak, showered, shaved, and dressed. Of course my attempts at being quiet failed and as I was tucking my shirt into my pants while easing myself out of the bedroom, Bette raised her head from the pillow and asked, "Are you all right?"

"I'm terrific. Just couldn't sleep. I'll feed myself and then probably take a walk."

She yawned. "I can't imagine where. . . ."

A thick mist was swirling close to the ground when I stepped out the front door and turned left on Blueberry Lane. Large tumbling clouds of vapor were still clinging stubbornly to the trees and boulders by the time I reached the pound and settled into my usual seat, which was a little damp. With moist daybreaks like this, I thought, it's no wonder that most of New Hampshire's unspoiled countryside is so lush and green.

Gradually, over the previous several weeks, the old pound had, indeed, become a special haven for me. In the dozen or so visits, despite my disappointment in not making contact with Simon, the pendulum of my mind seemed to almost come to a stop once I was within the confines of that unique place, and even hours after I had walked away I still felt completely relaxed, refreshed, and yet charged with high energy.

"Isn't it rather early for you, Mister Og?"

He was leaning against the stone wall directly opposite me and his smile was brighter than any sunrise. I surprised myself, remaining calm and seated and replying, without much of a quaver in my voice, "It's never too early, providing I can spend a few moments with you."

He smiled and nodded approvingly, moving slowly around the outside of the wall and finally seating himself close to me, as he had done on that first meeting. He extended his large right hand and I grasped it with both of mine.

"You have been such a busy man since our last meeting," he proclaimed admiringly in that deep bass voice that seemed to reverberate through the woods. "Speeches on the greatest secrets of success to huge crowds in Nashville and St. Petersburg and Sarasota, not to mention the long lines of your fans waiting to have your autograph in a Mandino book. And you have been gardening as well. Simplicity roses! And blueberry bushes! Just wait until you taste the fruit from that succulent Jersey variety. Mister Og, my frequent-flyer horticulturist! I am exceedingly proud of you."

Neither his great charm nor my respect and love for him was going to sidetrack me this time. "Simon, why did you vanish, after our last meeting, before I could introduce you to Bette? She was brokenhearted."

He sighed and patted my knee. "Mister Og, I wanted very much to meet your lady, but she is too nice a person to be handicapped by possessing firsthand knowledge of me. You know the many problems you have encountered, through the years, whenever anyone has asked you about me and our friendship. Why should we drag Bette into this unique association? Let her be able to say, forthrightly, to all who might ask, that she has never met me, and let the truth protect her."

"You seem to have a pretty good idea of what I've been doing for the past few weeks. Now, tell me, please, did you actually mean it when you said you've been monitoring my life for the past fifteen years?"

"Mister Og, I have watched over you because of my love for you. If anything happened to you of a harmful nature, I wanted to be informed of it immediately so that I could hurry to your assistance."

"Simon, please understand. I can't even find words to tell you how grateful I am for your concern, but I am struggling with all of my ability to understand what you are saying. Watch over me? That's a physical impossibility. The human mind, at least my puny one, just can't handle the kind of other-dimension activity you talk about so casually. What you say you have done with me is impossible. . . ."

Simon shrugged his broad shoulders. "You, more than anyone, Mister Og, should know how little in this world is actually impossible. You write on that subject so often. Perhaps you might like to test me. Why not give me some small clue, some tiny fragment of an incident, either major or minor, from your past fifteen years, and let us see if I can fill in the details for you."

I was certain I would stump him with my very first challenge. Only a few close friends were aware of this interesting but relatively insignificant event from my past.

"Imelda Marcos!" I said smugly.

He nodded approvingly. "Very good choice. It seems that several years ago you were in Manila to promote your books. After a full morning of several radio and television shows, you and Bantam Books' international sales manager, Robert Michel, returned to the Manila Hotel, where you were both staying, for a brief rest and lunch before the afternoon appointments began. Your telephone was ringing as you unlocked your hotel door and so Mr. Michel, being as protective as possible, stepped in ahead of you and picked up the telephone receiver. As he held the phone to his ear you could see that this very bright man was now frowning and had turned slightly pale as he continued to repeat, 'Yes, sir . . . yes, sir!' Finally he said, 'We'll certainly be there, sir' and as soon as he hung up he broke into a fit of laughter exclaiming, 'You are not going to believe this, Og, but that was the palace calling. It seems that the president's wife, Imelda, saw you on television this morning and she was very impressed. She has extended an invitation to you . . . and I'm permitted to accompany you . . . to lunch at the palace.' You, Mister Og, were not pleased. You were waving your afternoon schedule at Mr. Michel and saying, 'Bob, we can't go to the palace. We have a bookstore autograph session in less than an hour.'

And Mr. Michel replied, 'Og, when the palace calls, you go.' The two of you did go and had a wonderful time and Mrs. Marcos had her wish."

The old man had not erred on a single detail. I tried a different approach and said, "1983?"

"That was truly a vintage year for you, Mister Og. You were awarded the first Napoleon Hill Gold Medal for literary achievement, and you also received the coveted CPAE Award from the National Speakers Association, which is the group's highest award for public speaking. Then, in 1984, you became only the fourteenth individual inducted into the International Speakers Hall of Fame, joining a distinguished group of orators such as Red Motley, Richard DeVoss, Bill Gove, Cavett Robert, and Norman Vincent Peale."

I wasn't about to give up. "Last September . . . the Cathedral of Notre Dame?"

He raised his head and gazed up at the pines and maples. Finally he replied, "You and Bette were with the Warren, Michigan, Church of Today tour group. As the huge throng moved on, following their guide through the crowded old church, you paused to light a candle in memory of your mother and father and when you arose from saying a brief prayer there were tears flowing down your cheeks. As you started forward to catch up with Bette and your group, you happened to glance off to your left and saw the Church of Today's fine minister, Jack Boland, standing perhaps twenty feet away, watching you and nodding his head with compassion and tenderness. Then you both waved at each other. It was a special moment, in a special place, was it not, Mister Og?"

Now I was certain I could trap him. "How many candles did I light, Simon?"

He never hesitated. "You attempted to light two, one for each parent, and you had inserted a ten-dollar bill in the locked brass box to pay for two candles. However, after you lit the first, try as you would, you could not get another candle to flame. Then you told yourself that since your mom and dad had shared everything while they lived, they wouldn't mind sharing a single candle now . . . and you moved on."

No one could have known my thoughts about my parents sharing a single candle. I didn't think I had ever even related that incident to Bette.

"How about this one? Several years ago, when the Spanish editions of my books, published by Editorial Diana in Mexico City, became available throughout Central and South America, I was invited to speak in many countries south of the border. What did the Honduran Ministry of Defense do for me during my visit to their capital?"

"Of course, Mister Og, they were rightly concerned about your safety and so they provided you with a twenty-four-hour armed guard from the moment you arrived. Two soldiers were always in your company, everywhere, making you rather uncomfortable when you went shopping or visited a restaurant. They even slept outside your hotel room in Tegucigalpa and they jabbered all night, rather loudly, reducing your sleeping time, did they not?"

"What hotel?"

"The Hotel Honduras Maya. And, Mister Og, you were very kind to the young armed men accompanying you. Do you recall that you always sent your waiter over to their table and insisted that they eat . . . as your guests?"

I just shook my head. "Let's try again. Golf . . . and South Africa?"

The old man chuckled and placed his hand to his mouth as if he were relishing the details of this particular episode. "The popularity of your books throughout the world has been a publishing miracle, Mister Og, and not too many years ago you went on an extensive speaking tour in South Africa. Apparently word had preceded your visit that you were an avid golfer and so those people sponsoring your appearance in Durban arranged a golf match for you on your free afternoon. Your sponsors thoughtfully supplied you with the proper size of golf shoes, decent golf clubs—Hogan radials, before you even ask—plus a caddy, and a great many members of the local press as well as a television crew were on hand. You were a little disappointed when you were first introduced to the other three members of your foursome, since they were all women, although you tried to conceal your feelings, but your whole attitude changed rather abruptly after the three ladies teed off on the first hole and each of their drives traveled at least two hundred and fifty yards . . . all well ahead of your ball. Of course, it did not take you very long to realize that some practical joker had paired you up with three of the finest lady professional golfers in the nation. Luckily for you, the three had insisted that the wagers be rather small, before driving off that first tee, otherwise you might have left a great part of your hefty speaking fee in Durban."

"Simon, several years ago when Bantam Books published *Og Mandino's University of Success*, I appeared on many radio and television shows across the country. One of them was the *Today* show. I was sitting offstage, fifteen minutes before I was scheduled to go on, when Jane Pauley came over to me and said something. What did she say?"

Simon grinned. "How many in the entire world would know, Mister Og?"

"Only Jane and I. Maybe I told Bette later. Three people, tops."

"Well, that very pretty lady had a small sheet of paper in her hand and she said she was going to review with you the questions she would ask when you two went on the air coast to coast. You thanked her and then surprised her by saying that you didn't need to hear the questions since you were pretty sure you could come up with a few interesting answers. She was surprised at your response, which she said she didn't hear very often, but she agreed."

"How did I do?"

The old man never lied. "You did fairly well," he said, rubbing his hands together gently.

I was still in there swinging. "Simon. Two months ago. The second of March, to be exact. What happened?"

"You and Bette flew to Phoenix, where on that Saturday night you spoke on behalf of the Seventh Step Foundation to a packed crowd at the Arizona Biltmore. What made this evening so special for you is that before you spoke, a proclamation was read, issued by Arizona's Governor Rose Mofford, proclaiming that very day Og Mandino Day in Arizona. You must have been exceedingly proud."

"I was. Now tell me, Simon, what was the gentleman's name who read the proclamation?"

The laugh started deep in his throat, and when he had finished he wiped his eyes carefully, shook his head, and replied, "Why, it was your old friend, the very best talk-show host in all of Phoenix, Pat McMahon!"

I didn't know what to say and so I remained silent. Finally Simon rose and placed his hands on my shoulders, stooping just enough so that he could stare directly into my eyes.

"Enough?"

"Enough," I answered.

"Mister Og, I realize how busy you are, but you and I should make every possible effort to meet again . . . and soon. I am certain that we can both profit through our meaningful discussions, as we have in the past, and it is my fervent prayer that we talk on a regular basis . . . perhaps even once a week. There is much ground for us to cover together. The world is in a terrible quandary and perhaps you and I can help as we did before. Would I be too presumptuous if I suggested that we might try to meet each Tuesday morning at nine? Is that inconvenient for you?"

"Tuesday at midnight would not be inconvenient where you are concerned, dear friend. This coming week is a very busy one for me but I will still make it next Tuesday at nine."

"Wonderful! Here? In this ancient pound we have adopted?"

"Perfect."

"What a magnificent location for us, Mister Og. We have both done our share of rescuing and reviving those who were lost and defeated. Me with my muscle and patience and wide shoulders and you with your books and your spoken words of hope and guidance and here we are, after all these years apart, finally coming together again in a unique place that was actually built, long ago, to harbor and protect some of God's creatures that had gone astray. How fitting."

I started to reply but caught myself in time. Telling Simon that I believed God was now playing chess with both of us did not seem to be the wise thing to do.

VII

By the time I arrived at the pound on the following Tuesday morning, Simon was already sitting on the lower stone wall that faced Blueberry Lane, arms folded, his unlit corncob pipe hanging loosely from a corner of his mouth. He was wearing an oversized, bulky knit white sweater with its collar up, and he turned and smiled when he heard me approaching.

"Look around you, Mister Og," he said, waving at the grapevines edging their way up the stone sides of the pound and the thick clusters of tiger lilies in bud near the road, "as Benjamin Franklin once said, 'The morning hour has gold in its mouth'!"

I tried to hold my own in the quote department by replying, "Now, dear friend, inhale deeply. As Milton wrote, 'Sweet is the breath of morn. . . .'"

He nodded approvingly and said, "You, of course, are familiar with one of New Hampshire's greatest sons, Daniel Webster . . . superb orator, attorney, politician?"

"Of course."

"Well, one day, perhaps after a difficult period in our nation's capital plus a longing for his country roads back here, he wrote the following: 'The morning itself, few inhabitants of cities know anything about. Among all our good people, not one in a thousand sees the sun rise once in a year. They know nothing of the morning. Their idea of it is that it is that part of the day which comes along after a cup of coffee and a piece of toast. With them, morning is not a new issuing of light, a new bursting forth of the sun, a new waking-up of all that has life from a sort of temporary death, to behold again the works of God, the heavens and the earth; it is only a part of the domestic day, belonging to reading newspapers, answering notes, sending the children to school, and giving orders for dinner. The first streak of light, the earliest purpling of the east, which the lark springs up to greet, and the deeper and deeper coloring into orange and red, till at length the glorious sun is seen, regent of the day—this they never enjoy, for they never see it. I never thought that Adam had much the advantage of us from having seen the world while it was new. The manifestations of the power of God, like his mercies, are new every morning and fresh every moment. We see as fine risings of the sun as ever Adam saw; and its risings are as much a miracle now as they were in his day—and I think, a good deal more, because it is now part of the miracle, that for thousands and thousands of years it has come to its appointed time, without the variation of a millionth part of a second. I know the morning, I am acquainted with it, and I love it. I love it fresh and sweet as it is—a daily new creation, breaking forth and calling all that have life and breath and being to a new adoration, new enjoyments, and new gratitude.' Imagine those sensitive and lovely words, Mister Og, coming from such an outwardly tough man as Webster."

"Simon Potter, you continue to amaze me!"

"If I read something and it touches me deeply, I will file it in my heart. In your most recent book, *A Better Way to Live*, you have a very poignant chapter about you and a black cabbie in Nashville. Would you like to hear me recite it verbatim?"

"No, no . . . I believe you!"

"Tell me, how did you enjoy your fiftieth high school class reunion last Saturday night?"

That type of question, coming from him, no longer even surprised me. "It was a terrible letdown, a great disappointment, a downer. I had been looking forward to that special night for many months because I hadn't seen any of my fellow graduates since that day back in June 1940, when we all walked off the stage at Natick's Colonial Theatre with diplomas in our hands. My mom died a couple of months later, I went off to war, and I really never returned to Natick after the fighting ended. Now here I was trying to mix with a roomful of strangers who all seemed very old, very weary, and very melancholy. So many of them, I learned as the evening wore on, had never really ventured very far, in their entire lives, from that nice little town where we grew up and went to school."

"Were they pleased with your great success?"

I laughed. "Simon, it was a wonderful lesson in humility, and I guess I needed it. Only a small handful knew anything about me or had read any of my books or had heard me speak or had ever seen me on television. Many times during the evening—and since Bette was with me she really got a kick out of all this—some unfamiliar face would come up to me, we would lean forward to check each other's name badges, make small talk for a minute or so, and then I would be asked what I had done with my life. I was tempted more than once to say that I had just been released after serving a long prison term or confide that I was still running the largest illegal gambling operation in East Boston. . . ."

"And how did you actually respond?"

"I just told them I was a writer."

The old man's laugh echoed through the woods as he slapped his knees. "A writer? Like Greg Norman is a golfer . . . and . . . Frank Sinatra is a singer!"

"Only you would say that. Thank you. Two or three times during the evening I met ladies whom I had been madly in love with at some stage of my high school career. After exchanging a memory or two with each of them I would thank God, silently, that my bashful and inexperienced advances, back then, had not led to anything serious and permanent. All in all, Simon, a depressing evening. It was truly sad to remember the bright and smiling faces of 1940 and realize that they had been replaced, with only a few rare exceptions, by tired and dispirited souls projecting little more than a somber look of forlorn hopelessness in all their actions and words. Most of them, it seemed, were just waiting to be buried, because their lives were already over. I was so happy to finally get out into the fresh night air."

Simon nodded. "Are you familiar with the name Gian-Carlo Menotti?"

"Of course. Christmas . . . television . . . *Amahl and the Night Visitors.*"

"Yes. Once this brilliant composer, teacher, motion picture director, and television playwright said that hell begins on that day when God grants us a clear vision of all that we might have achieved, of all the gifts we wasted, of all that we might have done that we did not do."

"And I can't think of a worse kind of hell, although I'm sure that most of my classmates, like the population in general, have no idea what they might have achieved with their lives. However, despite a rough Saturday night, the trip down to Massachusetts was not a total waste. On the day following the reunion dinner, Bette and I went to tea at the house of a very special friend and classmate at Natick High, Jean Foley. Jean, despite several bumps on her road of life, had raised a lovely family and was still the dynamic, vivacious firecracker I had known so long ago. After visiting with Jean, Bette drove for several blocks, following my directions, and suddenly it was in front of us . . . the old athletic field, Coolidge Field, where Natick High had played its football and baseball games and conducted its track meets half a century earlier. Although there was now a new high school and stadium, several miles away, Coolidge Field was still in excellent condition and was obviously used frequently by local baseball teams. I asked Bette to stop the car, stepped out, and walked through the open wire fence gate as she remained in the car and watched with a puzzled look on her face. At the far end of the field, two young boys were playing catch, and off to one side, where the old wooden grandstands had once stood, a portly man was trying to chip yellow golf balls in the direction of a red straw hat that lay on the ground perhaps fifty yards away. Suddenly, and I don't know what got into me, I began to jog along what had once been the back-stretch of the quarter-mile track that had surrounded the field. I picked up speed a little when I hit the far corner. Fifty years earlier that had been the place, close to where the varsity baseball team's home plate had been located, where I would always shift into high gear in my quarter-mile races. I continued running, turned into what had been the final hundred-yard straightaway to the finish line, and accelerated my speed as best I could, racing all the way to where white tape indicating the finish line had always been strung across the track—white tape that I had been fortunate enough to break, in victory, several times during my senior year. Out of breath, I walked wearily over to the tall fence, passed through the gate, looked back at my own field of dreams, wiped a few tears from my eyes, and jumped into the car. Bette never said a word, bless her heart."

Simon's voice was nearly a whisper when he asked, "Mister Og, do you recall what you managed to accomplish on that very field during the afternoon of the second of May in your senior year? On that day, after rain had delayed your high school's track meet with the Wayside Inn School for several hours, you proceeded to accomplish a feat that has never been matched since then by any of your school's legion of great athletes . . . you were victorious in the hundred-yard dash, the two-hundred-and-twenty-yard dash and . . . the quarter mile! A triple victory!"

"I remember all three races. And I've still got some old and faded newspaper clippings somewhere. You know, Simon, looking back on that reunion, I believe the toughest part for me and probably for all the others was accepting the fact that fifty years had passed. Being with all my elderly classmates and seeing my reflection in them drove it home, very forcefully, but it still seems to me as if graduation was only last month."

"Mister Og, let me help you put it all in proper perspective. During the year that you graduated, Jack Dempsey retired from the ring, the very first Social Security check in history was issued, this nation's population was only half what it is today, the Dow-Jones Industrial Average was less than two hundred, the first-ever successful helicopter flight was made, new Fords and Plymouths and Chevrolets were selling for less than nine hundred dollars, and the big book was *For Whom the Bell Tolls*, by one of your favorite authors."

I remained silent and he continued. "The reunion journey was one you had to make. All children are innocently cruel to their peers, and because your beloved mother and father struggled so hard to escape the jaws of poverty, your classmates managed to inflict damaging wounds to your self-esteem by the time you had passed through twelve school grades and graduated. I recall you once telling me how envious you had been of the others, with their new clothes and spending money, while you had neither. At the reunion you were finally able to look at those same individuals through a different pair of eyes. I wonder how many other millionaires, self-made at that, were attending that function. I'm so glad you went."

"I am, too, after listening to you. Bette and I also made a long-overdue visit to the cemetery on Sunday and we both said our 'hellos' to my mom and dad. There are now far more gravestones in that section where they are buried than there were when I knelt and prayed and cried at their funerals so long ago. Neither of my parents is there, anyway, so far as I'm concerned. I've always felt that all I had to do, in order to talk with either of them, was just walk out in the backyard, look up, and speak."

Simon patted my head gently, as he had done so often before. "I am very pleased that you have finally returned to your roots. This unique state is a very special part of the nation and although New Hampshire has so much to offer, it remains one of the country's best-kept secrets. Did you know that almost ninety percent of this state's land is covered with trees . . . land on which there are nearly two thousand lakes and ponds, two hundred mountains that reach more than three thousand glorious feet into the heavens, as well as twenty miles of breathtaking coastline studded with scores of white, sandy beaches?"

"You truly are taken by this place where I expect to spend the rest of my life, aren't you?"

"In this blighted world of noise and crowds

and pollution and traffic, it is very close to heaven here, Mister Og. Glacial caves, berry bushes, white birches, fragrant pines, endless ski trails and downhill runs, apple trees everywhere, mind-boggling views from atop Mount Washington, America's widest main street in Keene, the two hundred habitable islands on Lake Winnipesaukee and, of course, the magnificent and miraculous display in early October when the leaves on thousands of maple trees explode in flaming reds and golds with touches of pink and plum and saffron, crying out to every autumn tourist to stop his car and take just one more photograph. Yes, my friend, I like your state and your land and your blessed home very much. You and Bette made a wise choice. You still have many productive years ahead of you in this peaceful setting, on this solitary dirt road, my friend, because here you will be blessed with the same two benefits that New Hampshire's great poet, Robert Frost, credited most for helping him to produce the very core of his writing. Are you familiar with Mr. Frost's work?"

"Yes. My favorite is the book *A Witness Tree.*"

"I have always been touched by his poem, 'The Gift Outright,' that he read at President Kennedy's inauguration. I believe I still remember all of it."

I chuckled. "I'm sure you do."

"When Frost was a young man, in his twenties, he settled on a farm in Derry, not too far from here, and he claimed that the ten years he spent there, doing considerable farming and some teaching, played a large part in his later successes as a four-time Pulitzer Prize winner as well as being honored as America's poet laureate. On the farm, he wrote more than half of his first book, portions of his second, and even some of his third, all destined to be published and praised later. The two benefits that made so much difference in the life of this brilliant man, during his years on the farm, were, as he once told a friend, the only things he had plenty of . . . time and seclusion. He admitted later that he hadn't planned things that way because his foresight was not that good, but the time . . . and the peace and quiet that enabled him to ponder and reflect . . . turned out to be the perfect ingredients in the shaping of his future. Time and seclusion, Mister Og, may well turn out to be the most valuable assets any of us can possess as we race frantically toward the twenty-first century."

"Well," I replied, shaking my head, "if your prediction is accurate, then I will truly be a man of wealth, because I'll certainly have plenty of both. When I look out my studio windows in January and see four feet of snow piled high outside, there won't be much else to do except put another log on the fire and another sheet of paper into the typewriter."

Simon smiled wryly and his eyes nearly closed, his usual pose when he was about to either tease or challenge me, as I remembered. "Perhaps, Mister Og, some winter day when you glance outside, you'll be greeted by the same shocking and unusual sight that befuddled every citizen of this area during the latter part of April 1933. Apparently it had commenced snowing after midnight and the snow fell so swiftly that there was almost three feet on the ground by dawn. This snow, however, was unlike any snow anyone had ever seen before in any part of the world! It was blue! Blue snow . . . and since the temperature was in the forties during most of the following day, the blue snow did not remain on the ground very long. To this very day there has never been any sort of explanation put forward, either by our government or by scientific circles, to explain the mystery, and so far as expert meteorologists attest, that single snowfall was the only one in the entire recorded history of the world that was blue! Maybe you can use that strange and rare event in one of your books someday."

Bingo! Jackpot! This was the moment! I would never have a better opportunity than right now. For my own peace of mind, and Bette's as well, I desperately needed some answers from him. I tried to think of just the right words, but that didn't work very well and so I just let it spill out.

"Simon," I said, "I have loved you almost since the first moment that I saw you standing in that old parking lot in Chicago, and your influence on my life can never be measured. Twice now, in the past few minutes, you have made reference to my future. You said that I have many productive years ahead of me, which was why you were so happy to see me in this environment, and . . . just now you said that perhaps I might write about New Hampshire's blue snow in a book someday. Someday? How many 'somedays' do I have? For my peace of mind, as well as Bette's, will you please answer two questions for me?"

The old man stood, stretched his giant frame, and walked slowly through the thick ferns until he was leaning against the taller wall, opposite me. "First," he half-shouted, "you would like to know if, at my advanced age, I am still in the ragpicking business . . . still removing humans from dump piles and gutters and guiding them toward that shining path that leads to peace of mind, self-pride, success, hope, and happiness. The answer is that I am still in business . . . although I have cut back quite a bit on my activities. As to the second and far more important question you would like answered, I expect that you want to know why, after my seemingly unforgivable disappearance years ago, followed by my long and silent absence, I have suddenly reappeared in your life unless I have reason to believe that something terrible is about to happen to you and I want to be close by in order to do whatever I can to save a good friend. Am I correct?"

I nodded, once again feeling very helpless before his mysterious powers.

Simon returned to his seat next to me, reached down, plucked a tall fern, and stared at it intently as he twirled the delicate stem in his huge hand.

"Mister Og, your friend Thoreau once made a very wise observation bemoaning the great masses of people who are leading lives of quiet desperation. Their number has increased dramatically in this country since you and I first met, back in the early 1970s. How sad. There seems to be an epidemic of despair, frustration, and hopelessness sweeping across our land, and for so many the precious gift of life has become little more than a frightening sentence to eternal misery and tears. Almost every day, it seems, another exotic gadget, electronic or mechanical, is introduced to us, with each promising to make our lives easier as well as provide us with a little more precious time we can call our own. Instead, we are discovering that we need all those new and expensive machines in order to increase our productivity just to keep up with the crowd! Mother has now permanently joined father in the workplace, not to provide the family with a few of life's better things, but in order to prevent the household from falling deeper into debt. Meanwhile, of course, their lonely children try to fend, as best they can, for themselves. Also, after struggling through a long and hard day of toil and pressure plus the horrors of fighting near-gridlock commuter traffic, there is little remaining time or energy to be either a loving parent or a caring spouse. The results, of course, are tragic. Walk into any large high school, my friend, and it has been said that you will discover that half the student body are children of divorced parents . . . and that group of confused kids will be, I promise you, the debris on tomorrow's junk piles in many cases. I fear, Mister Og, that those who are truly living and enjoying the American dream are becoming an endangered species, because the world as we have known it is sadly vanishing."

I said nothing, trying to concentrate on his words so that I could recall them later. "Even fifteen years ago," he continued, "when we first met, there were not enough available ragpickers to rescue everyone who needed help and guidance in order to find the path that leads to pride and fulfillment. It is a far more serious problem today. Think of this terrible fact of life: On this lovely day, as we sit here in this idyllic setting, more than four million homeless are walking the streets of our nation, hungry and fearful for their safety, plus we have another million individuals behind bars. Unfortunately there is nothing I can foresee that will prevent this terrible horde of wasted humanity from increasing in volume and velocity in the years ahead. The few ragpickers who are available can always provide guidance for those who are under their care, but they certainly cannot deal with the epidemic of nationwide proportions that threatens us."

He paused and focused those handsome brown eyes intently on me to make certain he had all of my attention. "Mister Og, just as the Salk vaccine prevented millions from suffering the crippling effects of polio, we are now desperately in need of some means of swiftly ending this great epidemic of failure and hopelessness. I am just one lonely ragpicker, and yet I finally decided that someone had to do something and that someone was me! I had nothing to lose by trying and a world to save if I succeeded, but you must understand that it was a difficult decision because of my advanced years. Despite all your kind words about how well I look, I realized that I had already far outlived most normal lifetimes and had little time to waste in completing my mission. And so, with all that on my mind, I journeyed here to New England, more than a year ago, seeking a quiet, isolated place where I would be able to completely concentrate my attention on all my years of experience in salvaging humanity. My goal was to develop a different kind of cure . . . a wonder drug of very few words, if you will . . . that would contain the simple and most powerful ingredients needed to prevent anyone from becoming infected by self-doubt and futility while guiding them, through the power of their own mind, to discover the satisfaction and peace and renewed self-esteem that had always eluded them."

"Why did you choose New England . . . and why a back road in New Hampshire?"

"Because of you. I remembered how lovingly and longingly you had always described this beautiful heaven on earth whenever we would talk in Chicago. If you loved this land so much, I knew I would, too."

Simon put his palms together and clapped several times. "And so," he continued, "in my travels I finally tarried here in Langville one day, was immediately captivated by the back roads and red maples, and luckily was able to locate a comfortable cabin that has suited me nicely during the past year while I have attempted to shape the lessons that life has taught me into a simple but effective medicine that anyone can swallow . . . anyone . . . in order to change his or her life for the better as the twenty-first century and also the third millennium approach us swiftly."

I was unable to conceal my deep sigh. "Then you haven't come here to rescue me from some terrible fate?"

The old man raised his right hand high. "I

swear to you that I was as surprised as you were when we found each other again . . . and elated as well, of course. Think about this amazing statistic, if you will, dear friend. In a single square mile of land there are more than seventeen thousand plots that measure forty by forty feet, which I would say is the approximate measurement of this old pound. Now, there are three million six hundred thousand square miles in the United States, or more than sixty-two billion plots of land the size of this enclosure. What are the odds of you and I meeting here, after fifteen years of no contact, within this single, particular, tiny, forty-foot-square stone compound? More than sixty-two billion to one! Quite a lottery payoff, I would say. No, Mister Og, your moving so close to me can only be a miracle . . . nothing else . . . as well as an answer to my prayers."

"Your prayers?"

"Yes, I do exactly as you do when I am confronted with a situation I cannot handle. I try to find a private place, get down on my knees if practical, put my hands together, look up, and simply say, 'I need help.' It has always worked for me in the past . . . and it worked this time! Mister Og, I know exactly what to tell people and how to advise them so that they can change their lives for the better but . . . but . . . during the long and lonely months here I have discovered a sad truth about myself. At my age I am no longer capable of putting my thoughts down on paper so that they radiate with the same power and clarity that they had years ago."

"I don't understand. You speak as beautifully

and coherently now as you ever did back then and there's certainly nothing wrong with your memory. Writing should be easy for you."

He sighed again and shook his head dejectedly. "Trust me, Mister Og, it is not . . . and I am afraid that my mission here may be in danger of failing. I hope, for old times' sake, that you will grant me a special favor and come visit me at my cabin next Tuesday instead of meeting here. It is not far. You merely continue down Old Pound Road for perhaps two hundred yards and turn right on the narrow worn path. Follow it and you will be led right to my door. Will you come, Mister Og, please?"

"Of course I will. I'm honored at your invitation. Thank you."

He grasped the wooden cross that hung freely from the leather cord around his neck and sighed. Then he reached over and gave me a gentle hug. "No, no . . . I thank you! Thank you! I was quite certain I could count on you, for I truly need your help."

Simon Potter asking *me* for help?

Now *that* was a miracle!

VIII

Beginning late in the spring, when the wild-flowers emerged from their long hibernation in all parts of our woods and meadow, I became very frustrated at my ability to identify by name only a few of those tough floral vagrants of Mother Nature, and so I spent long and intense hours, as if I were researching a book, poring over several field guides in order to recognize and better understand the wildflowers of New Hampshire.

Tuesday morning, on my way to visiting Simon at his cabin, I discovered several clusters of fragile starflowers, with seven graceful white petals serving as the perfect setting for their long golden stamens. Close to them were perhaps a dozen clumps of Indian pipes, with their pale, translucent stems and graceful, nodding heads rising from the leafy embankment along the north side of Blueberry Lane. When I finally found the narrow path that Simon had described, leading off Old Pound Road, I was surrounded by masses of fireweed, with their spikelike clusters of deep pink flowers rising nearly to my eye level. I walked forward slowly, with arms extended, so that I could gently push aside the sturdy stems of these tall and haughty beauties without harming any of them.

Since our section of Langville rises several hundred feet above the surrounding countryside, there is usually at least a gentle breeze that one becomes accustomed to feeling and even hearing as it flows through the trees. However, on this bright and sunny morning there was not even the slightest hint of air movement, so that the usual constant fluttering of leaves was absent. In the silence, I suddenly became aware of a strange and fascinating chorus . . . buzzings and hummings . . . squeals and squeaks . . . chirpings and soft moans . . . all low-decibel sounds that one rarely hears, of insects and birds and tiny animals and Lord knows what else, hidden beneath the cover of nearby shrubbery, going about their normal daily routine. Another world . . . a fascinating world we are still trying to understand . . . and all just under my clumsy feet.

Simon's cabin was located just far enough off into the woods so that it was not visible from Old Pound Road. I had been expecting to find a sturdy cabin of logs, similar to so many that surround our lakes and ponds, and so my first view of the tiny shack, with its exterior sides covered only with loose gray wooden shingles, was quite a shock. Simon Potter certainly deserved better than this. He was standing in the doorway, waving and smiling as I approached.

"Welcome, old friend, welcome to my humble home. Come in, come in!"

Several old pines and a leaning birch crowded very close to the right side of the cabin and on the other side I could see that the old man was growing a fairly large vegetable garden. Recalling

86

the terribly congested area where my office and his apartment had been, I embraced him and said, "It is not quite Chicago, is it?"

"Chicago is a great city, Mister Og, but you are correct. It is not the same, thank God, and yet the problems of the big cities are rapidly catching up with us, even in this peaceful isolation. Did you know that huge outpourings of sulfur dioxide, spewing from power plants as far away as Illinois, along with vile nitrogen oxide from millions of car exhausts in eastern cities, is now raining down upon us here . . . here in Langville and all of New Hampshire? Clouds of deadly vapor constantly drift across the nation and then move up the eastern coastline, accumulating more and more tons of exhaust excrement on the journey, finally depositing it where? Here! Acid rain! Smog! Our trees are now dying in epidemic numbers, especially the red spruce. The big city has finally come to us and there is no place to hide anymore . . . no place!"

"Thoreau once said that in wildness is the preservation of the world."

The old man shook his head sadly. "If Thoreau were alive today he would be making very loud noises."

Simon followed me into the cabin and I came to a dead halt after only a few steps. "Wow!" I exclaimed.

He nodded, looking both proud and pleased. The cabin's walls were paneled in light knotty pine. Burgundy-colored drapes hung neatly from the four windows of the all-purpose single room the old man had made his home. A narrow bed stood against the front wall, flanked by book-laden nightstands with pewter lamps. Against the left wall was a large wicker sofa, and next to it stood a dark rolltop desk, closed, with a swivel chair. A gray enamel sink and stove were beneath the rear window, with a refrigerator nearby as well as a small table with two chairs, and the fourth wall was covered with floor-to-ceiling book-cases, packed with books, except for a closed door that I assumed opened onto his bathroom. A small blue Jotul wood stove squatted in the center of the room on thick red tiles, its silver chimney pipes reaching straight up to the wallboard ceiling and beyond. Next to the stove was a brass carrier filled with cut wood, and above the sofa hung several framed portrait engravings. Small braided rugs were on each side of the bed. The place was immaculate.

"Very little that you see are possessions of mine, Mister Og. All the furnishings as well as the bedding, china, and silver were here when I moved in. This cabin stands on a large parcel of land, along this western side of Old Pound Road, that is owned by a lovely and wealthy old lady in Francestown. Her only son spent many winters here while enjoying the fine skiing on nearby Crotched Mountain. Unfortunately, the lad was killed in an automobile accident near Rome, two years or so ago, and although she was reluctant to lease this place, she finally weakened after I employed all of my charm over a lengthy session of tea. It is perfect for me. Warm and cozy and quiet so that I am able to think and write."

"What do you do for supplies? Groceries?"

"It is only about a mile to the small convenience store in the upper village. The walk does me much good. I place my order with Mr. Hammond, the owner, and when he has an opportunity he delivers it all to me in his old pickup truck. I want for very little, my friend, and I still tremble at the astronomical odds of your moving within a ten-minute walk of here."

I pointed to the faded and chipped blue plastic double dish on the floor near the refrigerator that seemed to contain dry dog food in one basin and water in the other. "You have another dog?" I asked, recalling the old multicolored basset hound, Lazarus, who had been his constant companion in Chicago fifteen years earlier.

Simon lowered his head. "No, that old bowl belonged to Lazarus. I always kept it full for him, in Chicago, and I still keep it full . . . in his memory. Seeing it there during the day always gives me the comforting feeling that he's not very far away. Lazarus lived to the ripe old age of sixteen, and I did consider replacing him after his death, however, I finally decided that it would not be fair to the new basset because I would be expecting the same special and lovable qualities that I treasured in Lazarus and, of course, no two dogs are alike. That bowl is just my salute to an old comrade, Mister Og, although it is quite insignificant compared to the dramatic tribute you paid to your basset after he was gone from you. *The Greatest Salesman in the World, Part Two,* was a magnificent work, but the book's dedication to your dog, Slippers, was one of the most touching pieces I have ever read and I'm certain I can recite it, verbatim, for you."

"You're very kind. Not very many books are dedicated to dogs, and I certainly never expected the tons of mail I received from animal lovers, all thanking me for loving my long-eared companion so much . . . as if that had ever been difficult. Toward the end of his life, his rear hip sockets had degenerated so much that he could barely stand or walk, and I can still remember a night, back at our Scottsdale home, when I opened our kitchen door and let him limp out onto the deck surrounding our fairly large swimming pool for a breath of fresh air. After a few minutes I got careless about keeping an eye on him and he apparently got his fanny a little too close to the edge of the pool without realizing that he was flirting with danger. Suddenly his right hip collapsed and Slippers tumbled sideways . . . into the deep end of the pool! Simon, I can't swim a stroke and so I guess it's just called 'love,' because without even hesitating I jumped in—clothes, shoes, wristwatch, wallet, and all—and grabbed my floundering sixty-pound buddy, heaved him back up on the cement and then, somehow, managed to get myself out of the water and onto dry land, although I still don't remember how. When I went to bed I was still trembling."

Simon patted my shoulder. "So each of us, in our own way, endures our loss but cherishes the memories. Just as it should be."

I pointed to the four framed engravings hanging above the television set. Simon shook his head and smiled. "Not mine. They belong to the nice lady who owns this place. She assured me they were all more than a hundred years old."

I could easily recognize the portraits of Longfellow, Lincoln, and Emerson, but the fourth face had me stumped. I stood and walked closer to the square-jawed image staring at me with patient eyes while locks of dark hair tumbled down his wide forehead close to his right eye. He looked like someone I could trust but would never want to tangle with, under any conditions.

"Who's he?" I asked.

"Mister Og, shame on you. How can you be an official New Hampshire resident now and not know Franklin Pierce, the only man from this state who ever became our nation's president? I take it that you have not yet paid a visit to the Pierce homestead in nearby Hillsborough? If you haven't, you should. Do you know this man's history?"

I shook my head.

"Franklin Pierce was the son of a former governor and a brilliant young attorney. When he was only twenty-five he was elected to the New Hampshire state legislature; he became its speaker at twenty-seven and was elected to the United States House of Representatives two years later. He became the youngest member of the United States Senate at the age of thirty-three, rose to the rank of brigadier general during the Mexican War, and was elected president of the United States in 1852 at the age of forty-eight."

Simon glanced up at me and cocked his head, making certain that I was paying attention. I nodded and he continued. "The story of Franklin

Pierce is one of the most heart-wrenching in American politics. Under different conditions in his personal life he might have been one of our greatest presidents and quite possibly have even prevented the terrible tragedy of the fast-approaching Civil War, because he certainly had the necessary amount of brains, courage, and integrity to deal with any challenge, no matter its size and gravity . . . except one . . . the terrible loss of everyone he loved . . . one by one.

"Two years after Franklin married Jane Appleton, in 1834, they had a son, Franklin, who died three days after his birth. Seven years later their second son, Robert Frank, expired from typhus when he was only four."

The old man paused and closed his eyes, wincing as if merely speaking the words was causing him pain. "Two months before his presidential inauguration, Franklin, Jane, and their only surviving son, eleven-year-old Benny, boarded a train in Andover, Massachusetts, for their home up here in Concord. They had traveled little more than a mile when an axle snapped and the train plunged down a deep embankment. Little Benny was killed before his parents' eyes. Now Franklin had to deal with this terrible tragedy and minister to a wife who seemed to have lost all vestiges of her sanity as well as prepare himself to lead our nation. Jane Pierce refused to accompany her husband to Washington for his inaugural, and after he was sworn in, despite his broken heart, he delivered an eloquent and masterful address without ever referring to a single note.

"Jane seldom ventured out into public, and as

the new president struggled each day with the heavy responsibilities of his office, he received little encouragement and support from a now very mentally disturbed wife who spent most of her waking hours in her room writing letters to her dead son, Benny. Jane, for all intents and purposes, had become as lost to her husband as his three dead sons. She never forgave her spouse for Benny's death. God had permitted little Benny to die, she reminded him at every opportunity, so that his father could concentrate on being president."

The old man inhaled deeply. "Mister Og, it has always been nearly impossible to serve this nation as its leader, with all the awesome responsibilities involved, unless one has a very special spouse to lean on for constant support and encouragement. Franklin Pierce, of course, had no one, and the man who was so strong-willed, spirited, and gutty gradually lost all semblance of those qualities along with his once-powerful drive and confidence. Problems over slavery were already beginning to erupt in violence in many states. Talk of civil war was everywhere, and yet our nation's leader showed no willingness or ability to deal with the impending crisis. He hedged his decisions. He vacillated. He compromised whenever possible. The man of such great promise, the man without a family, had now grown timid and weak, and his party rendered the final blow, the very worst of insults, refusing to nominate him for a second term . . . a very rare event in American politics."

Simon returned to the sofa, sat at my side, and

sighed deeply. "Franklin Pierce returned to Concord a broken man and watched, in helpless pain and guilt, as the nation he loved drifted toward war . . . a war that he might have been able to prevent had fate not destroyed his potential for greatness. Until her death, a day rarely passed when Jane failed to blame her husband for Benny's terrible death. Instead of being the fine president he could have been, his record is one of the worst. What a terrible waste! Jane passed away in 1863 and her still-loyal spouse, who had nurtured, protected, and loved her for almost thirty years, saw that she was laid to rest next to her three sons. Franklin joined them . . . six years later. There were few mourners."

A small pendulum clock on the top shelf of a bookcase was ticking loudly and, outside, I could hear a crow calling. After several minutes of silence, I asked, "Simon, could you have made a difference in that man's life had you been around in those days?"

"I believe so. In the case of our nation's first family, of course, the major difficulty is in establishing contact with them. Had they been my assignment I would have devoted most of my time and effort toward attempting to counsel Jane. Helping her to accept the past that she was powerless to change might have given her the strength to face the future with hope and anticipation instead of terror. If Jane's attitude had been altered, such a terrible weight would not have fallen on Franklin's shoulders and perhaps if help had been given her early in his term a different sort of president might have been strong enough

to avert so much heartache . . . for himself and
our nation. Of course it is easy to point out these
possibilities with hindsight. In truth, Mister Og,
no one knows what might have occurred if an
earlier-generation ragpicker had been dispatched
to the White House."

Simon rose and walked slowly across the
small room, pausing with one hand on his closed
rolltop desk. He lifted gently and the top slid up,
disclosing an interior stuffed with papers and
projecting ends of yellow legal pads. "Mister Og,"
he said as he leaned against the old desk, "I
believe that in your writing career you have
served as coauthor on two books, have you not?"

"Yes. I coauthored a book called *Cycles: The
Mysterious Forces That Trigger Events* with Professor Edward Dewey, founder of The Foundation
for the Study of Cycles, and later I wrote *The Gift
of Acabar* with Buddy Kaye, a gifted lyricist of
many hit songs including 'Till the End of Time.'"

"And how did you collaborate with them in
putting those two books together? What was your
role?"

"Actually, quite similar in both cases. Professor Dewey sent me half a truckload of his papers
dealing with his findings on cycles in the weather,
stock market, sunspots, and hundreds of other
diverse phenomena of man and nature. I spent
more than a year reading and reducing this often
technical material into a simple book, in my own
words, that an average person could read and, we
hoped, enjoy about this very fascinating subject.
Then I sent the manuscript to Dewey, he made
many suggested changes, returned it to me, I

rewrote the whole thing, sent it to him again, he approved, and it was published. Professor Dewey, bless him, is no longer with us, but I understand that his foundation, now based in California, is still selling our book, twenty-five years after it was first published. In Buddy Kaye's case, he wrote me with an idea for a story about a young lad in Lapland who flew a giant red kite, caught a star, and brought the star down to earth, where it rested in a tree and talked to our young hero about life and hope and love. I liked the concept enough that I agreed to write the book, then sent it to Buddy for his suggested changes, worked them into the material, and my publisher, Bantam Books, bought the book. It is still available in paperback, after more than a dozen years."

"That is amazing, Mister Og. Most books vanish forever after a year or so, and yet all fourteen of yours are still being sold after all this time?"

"No, only thirteen are still being published. Once I wrote a tiny book called *U.S. in a Nutshell*, which helped explain all those large numbers we all must deal with every day. It got great reviews including, as I remember, a full page in the Sunday edition of the Baltimore *Sun*, but it wasn't promoted at all and that was before my name on a book meant very much, so it didn't sell well."

"Then you have actually produced a book that did not sell in the hundreds of thousands?"

"I certainly have."

The old man grinned as if he already knew and was just teasing me again. He sighed and pointed toward the mass of papers on his desk. "I have spent the better part of a year at this desk, and my respect for your profession is greater than ever. Last week I reviewed my notes and I believe I have just about covered all the necessary principles, and they are not many, that one must follow in order to alter the course of one's life for the better. I am convinced, Mister Og, that you have come to this tiny village for a reason, perhaps many reasons, even if you know not what they are. One of them, I hope, is to lend me your hand. Perhaps you might recall that a lady named Shirley Anne Briggs, also a fine writer herself, wrote you a letter several years ago where she stated that there is a land of despair and a land of faith . . . and the bridge between the two is hope. She then went on to tell you, my friend, that you are in the manufacturing business. The hope business. You give people who are in despair the link of hope with which to reach faith, and you do this with one of the most powerful tools God has given us, the gift of writing."

Although I've averaged more than a hundred letters a week for several years, I did recall that touching letter. How Simon knew about it I didn't even bother to ask.

Simon placed his hands on my shoulders and said, "Mister Og, all of my worldly goods, except for my beloved books, could be stuffed into one duffel bag, but I would still like to leave something behind of value, for all to share, in this world I love so much. Will you, sir, please contribute some of your great talent in attempting to halt this illness that is sweeping the world. Please help me to put together my guidelines for a better tomorrow. That will be my legacy, my bequest, my gift to humanity. Ideas, using very few words, and yet with the power to renew wasting lives."

"I would consider it a great honor to work with you. When shall we begin?"

"Soon, very soon. Perhaps in a month, or a little less, I will finally have this mass of notes rewritten so that you will be able to make sense of my terrible writing. At that time I will hand over all my work so that you can take my concepts and hard-learned lessons of life and shape them into a stirring manifesto with the power to affect every living soul who follows its directions."

"That's a tall order, old friend. I don't know. . . ."

Simon removed his unlit corncob pipe from the corner of his mouth for the first time. His eyes were moist. He inhaled deeply and bit at his lower lip. "You can do it, Mister Og. I am positive that you can and I would be so honored to be your coauthor . . . just once . . . before . . ."

It became very still inside the cabin. I didn't know what to say, but I finally asked, "Do you have a name for this life-changing treasure you and I are going to produce?"

He grinned sheepishly. "I was hoping you would help in that area. Your books always seem to have just the right title and I know that most of them are your own ideas, not something suggested by your publishers. Of course I have thought of many but none seem to have the promise and the love and the resolution that I feel is needed. Let me leave that to you, for now, and we'll see what happens. In the meantime, while I am assembling my writings for you, please let us continue to meet each Tuesday morning at our beloved pound. Of course my door here is always open to you, but there is a wonderful feeling of peace and love that seems to surround that little square of granite boulders up the road. Just be prepared to work your magic with words for me, perhaps in a month. Is that satisfactory?"

Before I could reply there was a loud thump, just above our heads, followed by something that sounded like an empty pop can rolling down the cabin's pitched roof until we heard it land on the crushed gravel that surrounded the front door. Simon continued to lean casually against his old desk, but he raised both arms to assure me that he knew exactly what was happening outside.

"I made a new friend several weeks ago and I believe he has returned, once again, to pay me another visit. Come outside, Mister Og, and I will introduce you two."

He was the largest bird I had ever seen in my life and he was standing close to the edge of the roof, head cocked to one side, studying both of us. A yellow and very lethal-looking bill protruded from a white head with a black stripe on the side of his crown, while most of the feathers on our visitor's back, sides, and stomach were tinted an almost luminescent bluish violet. He shifted his weight from one thin, greenish-brown, gangly leg to the other, again and again, and finally decided to spread his wings, which had to be at least five feet from tip to tip! A soft guttural sound continued to come from his throat as if he were trying to pronounce the letter *r*. Although he seemed to be standing on stilts with a head that was balanced on several feet of thin neck, he was still a lovely and graceful creature and he obviously had no fear of us.

"Mister Og, this is my very special friend. He is a great blue heron, one of the most beloved and respected species of birds in the entire world. Fortunately for us, there are still several nesting areas for these special creatures of God here in New Hampshire. This one has his summer nest in a beaver and lily pond less than half a mile from here, back in the woods, in the very top branches of a tall, dead oak that still stands erect out in the middle of the water."

"Look at the size of him! This is the male?"

"Yes. The female is slightly smaller but with the same plumage."

"And you two are friends?"

"I am proud to say we are. Several weeks ago, while I was taking my morning stroll, several miles into the woods I came across this wonderful specimen enmeshed in a thick tangle of wild grapevines. The most terrible sounds were coming from him, loud calls of obvious panic and fear, but as I approached him slowly, he suddenly ceased crying and struggling and began watching me warily. Not until I had moved to within a few feet of him did I become concerned about the damage he might do to me with his long, tough bill, but, almost as if he knew I was about to rescue him, he remained absolutely still and quiet when I began to hack away at the tough vines that held him, until he was finally free. I sat back on the ground and watched as he staggered to a standing position, opened his huge wings several times, looked at me with first one eye and then the other, walked away for perhaps twenty feet, looked back at me, and finally leaped into the air, soaring up through the trees and high into the heavens. I didn't expect I would ever see him again, since I make it a point not to go near the pond and disturb either the birds or the beavers."

"He is something special! Amazing! You probably saved his life, Simon."

Simon laughed. "And now I receive my reward, again and again. Nearly every day, my friend will circle the cabin for several minutes, land on the roof not too gracefully, as you heard, and release from his bill some shiny object he has discovered . . . a glass bottle, a tin can, an old comb, even a cowbell once. He will just stand up there, as he is doing now, until I acknowledge his gift, and I have even found him waiting patiently, if I am not at home, until my return. After I thank him, he flaps his giant wings and immediately departs. Watch . . . !"

Simon moved away from me and retrieved the empty aluminum can that the great blue heron had just delivered. The old man waved it at the bird several times and shouted, "Thank you, my special friend, thank you so much!"

I swear the bird nodded his head before he crouched, raised those awesome wings, and with a loud "swoosh" was gone.

I placed my arm on the old man's shoulder and said, "Simon, knowing you as I do . . . I'm surprised you haven't given your new buddy a name by now."

"Ah, but I have, Mister Og, I have. Even as I was setting him free from what might have been a terrible fate, I was already calling him Franklin."

IX

▬◄▬◄▬◄▬◄▬◄▬◄▬◄▬◄▬◄▬◄▬◄▬◄▬◄▬◄▬◄▬◄▬◄▬◄

The month of June was a very special gift from God. All of southern New Hampshire, for days on end, was blessed with bright azure skies except for small, harmless, cotton-ball–shaped clouds that paraded lazily overhead almost every afternoon on their way to the ocean. Although the temperature rarely reached eighty, the sun was dazzling and intense, casting a shimmering glow on everything touched by its rays, even grouchy humans. Soft breezes were heavy with the fragrance of pine and freshly mowed grass, while the nights were perfect for sleeping, sometimes even under a blanket.

Bette and I did our very best to take full advantage of our state on its finest behavior. Each Wednesday morning we would toss two suitcases into the back of our Grand Wagoneer and hit the road. On one trip we went in search of colonial antiques for our old farm, especially a wooden butter churn to enhance one corner of our newly refurbished Early American kitchen. We traveled east out of Concord and spent the day along Route 9 visiting at least a dozen antique shops and acquiring many age-weary items such as a battered tin-lined copper pan with lots of character, tall antique bobbins to be used as candle holders, a Wallace Nutting print, tin chocolate molds, wire trivets, even a small wooden school desk, but no butter churn. We stayed in an old colonial house near Durham for bed and breakfast, and during the following day we tried to visit every factory outlet in Freeport, Maine, from Calvin Klein to OshKosh B'Gosh as well as the mind-boggling, open-twenty-four-hours-a-day L.L. Bean store.

On another Wednesday we headed in the opposite direction, northwest across New Hampshire and all of Vermont until we arrived in the small town of Charlotte, virtually on Lake Champlain. In Charlotte is the Vermont Wildflower Farm, a thriving business offering various mixtures of wildflower seeds. After receiving their catalog, Bette and I had begun discussing the possibility of giving our meadow, which was rapidly being overrun with dense underbrush, a facelift. We spent most of the day at the flower farm among the six breathtaking acres of hundreds of varieties of wildflowers, many bursting into bloom in an unbelievable spectrum of colors from flaming red poppies to sky-blue cornflowers to drifts of wild white baby's breath to pink, white, and gold cosmos, and when we departed we were determined that "project wildflower" would be on next spring's agenda after a deep plowing of our meadow late this autumn.

On another trip we headed down to Boston and inched our way through terrible traffic just to sit in old Fenway Park, cheer for the Red Sox, and eat popcorn as I had done on a few rare occasions with my dad, back in the days when Joe Cronin was managing and playing shortstop and Jimmy

Foxx was hitting home runs in clusters over that friendly left-field wall. Of course there was a trade-off for that trip. On the following day, Bette went shopping on Washington Street and I had to carry shopping bags . . . full ones!

Usually we planned our excursions so that we'd be back at the farm on Friday evening. Saturdays and Sundays were spent relaxing on the long and comfortable deck that Curt and Edd had built at the rear of our house, either reading or having breakfast or lunch or just listening to the symphony of sounds from the nearby woods. On Mondays we usually did some grocery shopping or, if the larder was filled enough, I'd try to get in some golf, either at a short but tough little nine-hole course in Hillsborough, aptly named Angus Lea, or at one of the most beautiful twenty-seven-hole championship courses I had ever played in all my years of chasing that stubborn little white ball, Bretwood Golf Course in Keene. Usually I had no trouble finding someone very willing to take me on.

And then there were always Tuesdays . . . Tuesday mornings. Simon and I met at the old pound each week punctually at nine in the morning, and we always spent at least a couple of hours together. During the early moments of our first Tuesday, the old man reached down, picked up a small granite rock no larger than his fist, and placed it in my hand. "Mister Og, do you know what this grayish-green material is that covers one side of this stone?"

"Moss of some sort?"

He grinned and shook his head. "No, this is a

perfect example of how nature survives and even continues to flourish when man does not interfere. This tiny, scaly crust happens to be one of the most complex plants in the world. It is called lichen, and it has probably existed longer than man, although, since it does not fossilize, we have no idea where or how long ago it came into being. Lichen are perfect examples of symbiosis, the intimate living together of two dissimilar organisms in a mutually beneficial relationship. Here we could all learn a lesson, for actually you are looking at two kinds of plants, an alga and a fungus, existing together for each other's benefit. The fungus serves as a shelter for the alga, preventing it from drying out, so that it can produce carbohydrates that the fungus then uses for food. This unique organism is so tough that it has managed to grow where no other kind of vegetation exists, such as in the Arctic or on the floor of Death Valley. Lichen are used in the manufacture of litmus paper and as a dye in Harris Tweeds, but one of their most important functions continues to be the process of slowly turning rocks into soil on which all other plants can establish themselves. They are truly a miracle. The fungus and alga can only survive because of each other's sharing, and yet together they not only survive, they make this a better world for all of us."

I rubbed my fingers across the stone's rough aquamarine coating, which reminded me of something one might see on a frosted window pane. Tiny pieces flaked loose and floated to the ground.

"Look at these stone walls, Mister Og. As you can see, many of the boulders are covered with lichen. After a rainfall they will darken in color, since lichen absorb many times their body weight in water. A lovely wall of God's jewels! Lichen! Another creation that few of us ever appreciate."

The wide array of subjects that Simon touched upon seemed to be merely random thoughts such as one might introduce to make interesting conversation, and yet, from my previous experience with him years ago, I realized that he was only trying to help me understand his viewpoints so that I would be better equipped to project his thoughts and feelings when I finally settled down to write his guidelines for life. What continued to amaze me about the old man was his wide scope of interests as well as how on top of current events he always seemed to be. He would have broken the bank on a television quiz show like *Jeopardy!*

Simon's concern about what man was doing to the environment colored much of his conversation, because he repeated, again and again, that it didn't really matter very much how well we managed to change our lives for the better if we had no clean air to breathe or pure water to drink or unpoisoned land to farm. One foggy Tuesday morning, soon after we had exchanged greetings, he leaned forward from his boulder and asked, "Are you familiar with that giant craggy male profile in granite, north of us at Franconia Notch, made world famous by Hawthorne in one of his classics titled 'The Great Stone Face'?"

"Of course."

"Did you know that acid rain is rapidly eroding that unique natural wonder and now when brave workers climb down its craggy face to apply acid retardants, the granite actually crumbles in their hands? Already, the profile that inspired Hawthorne and Webster has changed considerably from their day and I dare not imagine what it will look like a century from now. By the way, Mister Og, would you like to hear what Webster wrote about that marvelous landmark?"

"Tell me."

Simon rose, raised his hands dramatically and his great voice once again thundered through the woods. "'Men hang out signs indicative of their respective trades; shoemakers hang out a gigantic shoe; jewelers, a monster watch; and the dentist hangs out a gold tooth. But up in the mountains of New Hampshire, God Almighty has hung out a sign to show that there He makes men!'"

In retrospect, I regret so much that I didn't bring one of my small tape recorders with me for our weekly sessions, although I'm not sure that Simon would have approved. I jotted down many notes, each week, as soon as I returned home, to preserve as much of what he said as possible.

After he had quoted Daniel Webster and rejoined me on the stone wall, he said, "Our factories are pumping so much toxic material and chemical waste into the air that there are now ten pounds up there for every human being in this country. Think of that! Industries in the state of Kansas, just to name only one of the fifty culprit states, are now releasing more than seventy thousand pounds of phosgene into the air each year. That terrible gas killed thousands when it was used as nerve gas during World War I!

"Mister Og, we now have four hundred million

automobiles in the world and they are spewing more than five hundred million tons . . . tons, I said, of carbon into the air we breathe each year. To compound the tragedy, it has now been estimated that unless drastic measures are taken soon, those emission figures will double within the next twenty years. Remember how nasty the air was in Arizona and especially around Phoenix during your last years there? As you already know, I'm sure, the dust and diesel soot as well as automobile emission poisons have become so severe a problem out there that those driving an automobile, from October to February each year, can only purchase special oxygenated fuels such as something called gasohol."

Simon peered up through the tree branches to the few visible patches of blue sky, sighed, and continued, "If heaven is above us, Mister Og, we are certainly blaspheming it with our most vile graffiti. Carbon dioxide and methane from the fuels we burn have been collecting above in a thick shell that is preventing our planet's heat from dissipating off into space, and so our temperatures down here are slowly but steadily beginning to rise. If they continue to ascend, disaster of a horrendous magnitude is inevitable. As the ice caps up north begin to melt, the rising oceans will eventually wash over and engulf all our great port cities, such as New York, New Orleans, Boston, Norfolk, and San Francisco; thousands of Midwest farms that form our nation's breadbasket will all become desert land, and lack of drinking water in areas such as Nevada and California will bring on horrors we cannot even imagine. Is all this just

so much doomsday double-talk? Judge for yourself. The five warmest years in our nation's recorded history, Mister Og, occurred in the past
decade. There are frightening consequences ahead,
for all of us, if we do not have the courage to act."

I learned so much more about the land we
were despoiling. Simon informed me that more
than seventeen thousand waterways of our nation
were contaminated; half of our six thousand dumps
would be filled and closed in the next decade; we
destroy more than half a million trees each week
just to print our Sunday newspapers; more and
more of our drinking water is becoming tainted;
fish, after living in waters both polluted and poi-
soned, are still not federally inspected in our
country; and more than half our nation's people
live in unhealthy areas that violate federal smog
standards.

At another of our Tuesday meetings, Simon
shifted his emphasis from what we were doing to
our Earth to what we were doing, or failing to do,
to each other. "Mister Og, did you know that in
this beautiful country of ours we are now murder-
ing each other at a faster pace than at any time in
our history—one murder every twenty-four minutes . . . twenty-two thousand a year! That the
weapons most used in these killings are firearms
of one type or another is easy to understand when
you learn that there are now nearly two hundred
million guns in private hands in this country. Is
that the way we truly wish to live? Do we all need
a revolver in order to survive here? I like that part
of your speech when you look out at your audience

and ask them what we are doing to ourselves . . . and then you cite some frightening statistics."

I couldn't help myself. "Simon, you even know what I cover in my speech?"

He grinned sheepishly and nodded. Then he stood, turned his back on me, raised his head as if he were looking out on a large audience, and quoted, almost verbatim, from the latest version of my keynote speech. . . .

"'What are we doing to ourselves? The number of heroin, cocaine, and crack addicts is growing too swiftly for us to tally, and we are now consuming more booze per capita than at any time in our history. More than three hundred thousand individuals tried to take their lives in this beautiful country of ours last year. That's an entire city! Each month, more than five million prescriptions are being written for Valium, and we are now treating more than four thousand new cases of mental illness every twenty-four hours. There *must* be a better way to live. There *is* a better way to live!'"

The old man turned and looked down at me apprehensively. "How did I do? Were those your words?"

He had been right on the button. I nodded helplessly and let him continue, regretting once more that I was not recording his perceptive commentary on our world. "Almost half a million students are dropping out of high school every year, and perhaps twice that figure are being allowed to graduate although they can scarcely read their names. Both the parents and our communities must share the blame for this sad situation that will come back to haunt us years from now. More than fourteen million children now live in poverty here in this land of plenty, and one out of every three employable blacks is not working. More trouble ahead! And can you imagine, Mister Og, that in spite of all the warnings from the most respected brains in medicine, we are still getting fatter, not thinner, and more than fifty million Americans continue to smoke! AIDS, that deadly disease, apparently a product of our generation, has almost reached epidemic proportions on our small planet. According to the World Health Organization, by the year 2000 there could be six million cases of AIDS in the world, and as many as three times that amount could be infected with the HIV virus."

Simon paused, and in a now so-familiar gesture he studied his clasped hands for several minutes as if he was gathering and organizing his thoughts. Then he stared at me and continued. "We are leading such a tense and uncertain life that in our concern for our own welfare we have ignored two very special groups of people, the young and the old. Nearly a million teenage girls become pregnant each year, the suicide rate for teens has doubled in the past thirty years, teenage arrests have increased by three thousand percent since 1950, and the leading cause of death among fifteen- to nineteen-year-old minority youths is . . . murder! We are planting terrible seeds for harvest. The problems of our old are just as serious. We are living longer now, Mister Og, as you and I have discussed before, and it has been estimated that more than thirty million old folks will be living alone early in the next century. Can you imagine what difficulties that situation will produce? Also, the Urban Institute in Washington has estimated that by then more than five million elderly will need institutional care . . . institutional care that at present is limited and so expensive that most who need it today cannot afford it. How sad. What is frightening is that these conditions will occur despite the fact that our government is already expending far more on the elderly than on all the programs devoted to the environment or education. Still, not enough! To make things even more complicated, our nation's face and bloodlines are changing rapidly. By the commencement of the new millennium, the year 2000, the greatest number of living Americans, for the first time in our history, will be descended from non-European stock."

Simon exhaled deeply and shook his head again. "The millennium. A thousand years coming to an end and a new thousand beginning. Did you know, Mister Og, that during the early weeks of the year 1000, as the last millennium began, terror gripped the people of most civilized nations who feared that the end of the world was at hand and that the Last Judgment was imminent? During the past thousand years, men and women have sometimes acted like beasts and on other occasions soared like angels. We have made astonishing advances in medicine and science and transportation and yet we still have little or no knowledge of how to get along with our neighbors or how we must think and act in order to change our lives for the better. Still, my friend, I have supreme faith that before it is too late, mankind will resolve its problems and begin to fulfill its true destiny by transforming this aching globe of ours into heaven on earth . . . a land filled with love and understanding for our youth, tenderness and caring for our old, food and shelter for the poor, sweet air to breathe, pure water to drink, good health for all, children laughing, birds singing, and every citizen of the world filled with pride. It is time, Mister Og, that we spend all our energies to recruit an army of ragpickers and first instill them with courage and confidence and pride in their own abilities and potentials. Then they can commence their missionary work, if you will, of guiding the masses in the repairing and rebuilding of our precious planet so that everyone . . . everyone . . . will be able to live a better life in the new millennium . . . and beyond. However, we cannot delay! Tomorrow may be too late. First we find our ragpickers, then we help them to convert their own lives into a force of power and success and happiness. Once they are imbued with confidence in themselves and their own abilities, they will then be equipped to lead the others in changing our world for the better. But . . . there is so little time. . . ."

Simon reached into his left jacket pocket and produced an empty pop can. Then he removed his unlit corncob from his mouth with his other hand and pointed the pipe's stem at the can. "This aluminum container was my morning gift from my friend, Franklin, the great blue heron. Mister Og, if I should toss this can into the woods behind us and no one disturbed it, how long do you suppose it would take to decompose?"

"I have no idea, Simon."

"According to the experts on these matters, at least a hundred years! It is my fervent prayer that with your help we will be able to compose a short but powerful message of resolve and guidance that will light the way for all those who want to be led along the path to a promising future . . . as well as inspire them, these ragpickers of tomorrow, to lead the masses in the rescue of our planet and its people . . . and I certainly pray that our words manage to survive at least . . . at least as long as this flimsy container."

X

Close to the woods behind our old farmhouse, and yet far enough from the pine boughs overhead so that they still received full days of sunshine, stood seven wild blueberry bushes, all taller than I am. By mid-July every branch, it seemed, was heavy with dark clusters of ripe berries, and since two of my most favorite pastries are blueberry muffins and blueberry pie, Bette and I had worked out a deal. If I picked them, she would do the baking, and so for several weeks I did my very best to keep my loving spouse close to her kitchen ovens.

This Saturday morning had produced an abundant harvest, nearly four quarts of luscious fruit, for which I made room in our refrigerator. Since Bette was on a shopping jaunt in Concord, I went into my studio and tackled an overflowing "In" basket. I had been waiting for a rainy day to deal with the mail, but not a single drop had fallen in more than three weeks, and I was beginning to feel more and more guilty about all the unanswered letters.

As always, it was not very long before I was deeply immersed in the contents of each envelope I opened, and I tried very hard to write the proper reply to letter after letter, whether it was merely a loving "thank you" for kind words of praise about one or another of my books or lengthier pieces of advice and counsel, based on my own experiences, for someone whose written message suggested that perhaps he or she was coming dangerously close to the breaking point in life. What always amazed and pleased me about nearly every letter received was the writer's tone of friendliness and openness. Since he or she had read a Mandino book, I was no longer a stranger, and so I was always being contacted as a respected friend.

I was in the long-overdue process of replacing a fading typewriter ribbon, after an hour or so of intense letter-writing, when there was a loud and frightening crash on the roof directly over my head. In seconds I was out of my chair and the studio, racing for the kitchen's front door, certain that a heavy dead bough that had been hanging precariously from the stately ash tree above our house had finally fallen. Out in the bright midday sun I took several steps on the front lawn before turning to look back toward my studio roof.

"Franklin," I yelled hoarsely at my surprise visitor after I had stopped laughing, "you have just got to start practicing those landings of yours! As an old Air Force cadet, I want to tell you that if they had a flight training school for great blue herons you would have washed out a long time ago!"

The giant bird raised his yellow beak and stared down at me rather disdainfully before shifting his long greenish-brown legs for better balance on the pitched roof. Then he extended his long neck in my direction, blinked several times, raised his magnificent wings, and departed without uttering a sound. I watched in awe as Franklin soared ever higher toward the north until his shrinking silhouette vanished behind the tips of several very tall oaks.

"Good morning, Mister Og!"

Simon Potter. I never saw or heard him approaching, but there he was . . . standing on our dirt road directly behind me, carrying a frayed brown briefcase in one hand while with the other he held on to a tall wooden staff for support. I ran across the lawn, reached out and embraced my old friend. "You have actually decided to come visit me? I can't believe it . . . and you had an escort!"

The old man smiled and nodded before removing his ever-present unlit corncob. "I promised myself, weeks ago, that someday I would have the joy of visiting you in your home, but I would not allow myself this great honor and pleasure until I had completed editing and gathering my findings about life and happiness so that you could commence putting them together for me . . . and for the world. I learned a long time ago that the best way to motivate myself to take on any difficult task or challenge is to promise myself a reward of some sort, but the reward would only be mine after I had completed that particular undertaking to my satisfaction. I had just departed from my house on the way here to visit you when Franklin appeared with another gift for me . . . this time a rusty screwdriver. After I extended my thanks to him and continued up Old Pound Road to the corner of your street, I noticed he was hovering low above me, and I wondered whether he would

117

accompany me all the way. I'm glad he did. Apparently he has accepted you, Mister Og, into his small circle of friends."

"I'm honored."

Pointing to the old briefcase Simon was carrying, I asked, "Does this mean you are ready to put me to work?"

"If you are still willing."

I put my arm around his waist. "I'm willing, if you are. Come into my house, dear friend. I'm sorry that Bette is not home. . . ."

Simon smiled. "I know. It is better for Bette this way."

As we entered the front hall, Simon paused and pointed to the guest book and pen that were resting on top of the apothecary chest. "I have never in my long life ever signed anyone's guest book."

I handed him the pen and opened the book. "Let this be the first."

"May I?"

"Please."

I moved alongside the old man and watched him write, in a flowing script that was almost calligraphy, *Simon Potter*. Next to his signature, where one would write one's address, he wrote *The Planet Earth*. After Simon placed his tall wooden staff in the hall corner and rested his briefcase against the wall, I took him on a tour of the whole renovated house, from the upstairs bedrooms and Bette's sewing room back down the stairway through living and dining rooms, kitchen and sun-room. At first I felt a little strange walking the old man into rooms that were larger than his entire living quarters, but he seemed to enjoy every minute of it and was especially fascinated by what Bette and I had christened our "Arizona Room." This was the huge, newly built room that son Dana had designed to hold our projection television set with its six-foot-wide screen, and it had been quite obvious to the both of us, almost from the beginning, that nothing we could possibly do would make such a room fit into the old country decor of the rest of the house. And so, from its dusty coral, beige, and Wedgwood-blue drapes, rugs, and wallpaper to its comfortable seating for ten, the room became a miniature theater with a southwestern desert aura accented by kachina dolls, DeGrazia serigraphs and original watercolors, old branding irons, and hanging china plates from our Scottsdale home, plus the Arizona governor's proclamation, framed of course, declaring March third 1989, "Og Mandino Day." I even managed to find several large varieties of cacti in a Concord supermarket, of all places, and they were flourishing in a large brass container on the floor in one corner of the room beneath a large sepia-tone photograph of Arizona's late, great artist, Ted DeGrazia, inscribed to me. Simon was especially intrigued by the large television screen, and so I had him sit on my favorite couch, which was the most distant seat from the screen, and then I turned the set on. He said nothing and I don't think he blinked even once as he stared at the screen, listening to the noon news from a Boston station, with his mouth slightly open and a look of almost childish bliss on his face.

Finally he sighed, slapped his knees with his huge hands, rose, and said, "Mister Og, this is a very special home, and I am happy for you and Bette. If it were mine I'm not so certain that I would be able to tear myself away, as you so often do, to continue fulfilling your obligations for speeches and book autographings and radio and television appearances in so many faraway cities. Certainly you are no longer motivated by the need for money."

I smiled, thinking to myself that he already knew so much about me it was a good probability that he also had a good idea of my net worth.

"Simon, beloved friend, it's all your fault. You put me on this life course many years ago. I'm just trying to follow in your footsteps, but I'll never come close to being the ragpicker you are. I just keep trying and now and then something happens that would make you proud of me."

Simon leaned toward me and kissed my forehead, saying softly, "I know, Mister Og. You have learned the secret of happiness that wise men have been proclaiming since the beginning of time. Henry Drummond wrote that there is no happiness in having or in getting, only in giving; Seneca told us that he who does good to another does good also to himself, not only in the consequence but in the very act; and I believe it was Emerson who reminded all of us that the greatest gift we could give another was not gold or silver or diamonds but the gift of ourselves. There's that definition of altruism again, Mister Og . . . that unselfish devotion to the welfare of others. And have you noticed how much good flows back to you as you continue in your mission of aiding others?"

We had passed through the living room again

and were close to the front hall. I reached down for the briefcase that Simon had rested against the wall, placed it in his hands, and said, "One more room for you to see . . . my studio. Come with me."

Simon followed me through the dining room and kitchen, but he halted after he had taken only a step or two on the studio's heavy carpet. He turned very slowly from left to right, carefully studying the celebrity wall of autographed photos, the plaques and awards I had received, the comfortable couches near the two northern-exposure windows, the fireplace and walls of books and my large, cluttered oak desk. Then, placing his briefcase on the floor again, he stepped toward the first wall of photographs, hands behind his back, and walked slowly around the entire room, saying not a word. He paused before a framed newspaper article with its headline reading "The Greatest Self-help Writer in the World" and leaned over to study it closer. Then he straightened and said, in almost a whisper, "I cannot believe my eyes! Of course I was never in your Scottsdale studio, but in your book, *A Better Way to Live*, you described that special room in great detail."

"Yes, I did."

"But . . . but . . . this room, this studio here in your New Hampshire home . . . it looks exactly like the studio you described in that book . . . except that room was in Scottsdale!"

"Simon, when I was writing *A Better Way to Live* I wanted very much to make my readers feel comfortable with me in order to open their minds to accept my suggestions on how to live a better life. And so, in that book, I invited them into my home, sat them down in my studio in Scottsdale, and tried very hard to make them believe they were actually in my home by describing in painstaking detail almost everything in that special room where I had written nine books, even down to the tiniest souvenir from my past. Then, as you know, things began to happen, things I hadn't planned on, like a trip to Boston that ended in our buying this old New Hampshire farm. By the time *A Better Way to Live* was published, that Scottsdale studio no longer existed, because we had sold the house and moved here, and I felt very guilty about that chapter in the book . . . as if I were not being truthful to those who read that book and placed their trust in me."

Simon raised his right hand and waved it around the room, exclaiming, "And so you converted this old summer room into an exact replica of all that you described in your Scottsdale studio? That is amazing!"

"As closely as I could. This lovely room is somewhat larger, with a view of the woods behind the house that is priceless, and the large bookshelves that Dana designed are much nicer and more spacious, plus I now have a fireplace, but all the photos and keepsakes and memorabilia of my life are still on display on many of these shelves exactly as they were in Arizona."

The old man sighed and shook his head before walking slowly to the wall of photos, his tall frame bent almost double as he studied the signed photo of Charles Lindbergh, the platinum album of Michael Jackson's *Off the Wall*, with an engraved inscription to me, and the other framed photographs. Then, from the brass and onyx coffee table between the two couches, he picked up a silver, red, and white Bantam audiocassette package containing *The Greatest Salesman in the World*, waved it at me several times, and asked, "Do you recall the tremendous waves of emotion you experienced on that first day that you arrived at the RCA recording studios in New York City, back in 1987, to record this cassette with a cast of Broadway actors?"

"You even know what I was thinking and feeling on that particular day, years ago, and you still remember it?"

Simon shrugged and smiled.

"Okay," I continued, patting his shoulder and pointing to one of the couches. "Let's be comfortable, and then you tell me about my recording session in New York."

For several moments he assumed that familiar pensive pose as he sat, elbows resting on his knees, while he studied his clasped hands intently after he had removed his old pipe from the corner of his mouth and placed it on the table.

"First, Mister Og, we must go back to 1945. After serving your country well and having been separated from the Army Air Force, you arrive in New York City with less than a thousand dollars that you had managed to save in the service, and you rent a tiny, one-room walk-up apartment, just off Times Square, purchase a second-hand typewriter, and attempt to fulfill your dream—and your mother's dream for you—to become a writer. You fail. Nothing you write . . . short stories, articles, even fillers . . . is of any interest to the magazine people you call upon, and finally, with your funds running out, you abandon your dream and return, dejected and brokenhearted, to your native New England.

"More than four decades pass and now the year is 1987. You are in New York City again, this time to record an audio version of your great classic, *The Greatest Salesman in the World*, the first of many recordings you would make for Bantam. After breakfast at your hotel, the New York Hilton, you step out onto the Avenue of the Americas. It's a lovely morning and so you walk the eight blocks south to the RCA recording studios not far from the corner, on West Forty-fourth Street. By the time you reach your destination you are breathing a little harder, not from your walk but from the gradual realization that this street, West Forty-fourth, was the street on which you lived in 1945. Emotions you cannot even comprehend are welling up inside of you as you look down the narrow, dirty, traffic-choked street strewn with litter. Nothing seems to have changed in all the years that have elapsed since this was your neighborhood! Dingy bars, delicatessens, Chinese and Mexican restaurants, debris on the sidewalk and in the street, panhandlers in several doorways, and the old Belasco Theatre make it all seem as if you had journeyed back in time. The recording studio looks almost out of place with its polished glass doors and windows. Above the left door is the number one-ten. You try so hard to remember. What was the number of your apartment building? No luck. You glance at your wristwatch. You've still got fifteen minutes. There's time! You walk slowly, almost hesitantly, along the eroding sidewalk, heading toward Times Square. Finally you stop. You are standing in front of a dingy glass doorway, rusted and pitted, and above the door, in aged metal numbers, is one fifty-eight. This is it! This is where you lived and struggled so hard, so many years ago, and it's still here! You edge closer to the dingy glass, shade your eyes against the pane, and try to see inside. There they are! There on the wall are the familiar mailbox slots, just as you remember them, and there is the steep and narrow stairway, now carpeted. You step back and before you realize what is happening, tears are streaming down your cheeks! Forty years and more have passed! The world that had ignored you then now honors you. At that time, twelve books written! Twenty million copies sold! The Napoleon Hill Gold Medal for Literary Achievement, *Who's Who in the World*! Strangers pass and stare at the elderly gentleman who is crying in public. Finally you take a deep breath, wipe your eyes, and move slowly back up West Forty-fourth toward the studio. However, by the time you have reached its doors you are now laughing . . . aloud . . . and passersby are still staring. Life! It has suddenly dawned on you that . . . at least on one level . . . all your ambition and hard work has accomplished for you, during the past forty years, is to nudge you just half a block up the same street where you began your pursuit for the better life! Still, you look up at the blue sky above the tall, dirty buildings and whisper, 'Thank you, God!' Then you enter the studio and go to work."

I had been listening as if mesmerized. He hadn't missed a single detail!

125

"Who are you . . . really?" I asked before I could stop myself.

There was love and compassion and a little sadness in Simon's wide brown eyes as he stared at me momentarily before standing. "Let me deliver to you what I have put together of my notes so that you can go to work," he said, reaching down near my desk, where he had dropped his briefcase, before returning to his seat. He opened the old leather container and removed a thin batch of papers in various colors and sizes, placing them carefully on the coffee table. Then he stared at the pile for several minutes before turning to me. "It does not seem to be very much," he said softly, "as the measure of a lifetime of work."

I started to correct him, to remind him of the thousands of lives he had saved and helped to reshape, including mine. Instead, I remained silent. Simon Potter was now running our meeting and we both knew it. I just sat back on the couch and listened.

"Mister Og, if one is an observer of our world and its current inhabitants it is a simple matter to fall into the deepest throes of despair. Pollution, poverty, taxes, drugs, wars, disease, and increasing crime confront us hour after hour and day after day until hopelessness threatens to become a way of life for most of us. We must not capitulate! Despite the whirlpool of evil and failure and degradation that swirls around us and our children, we must never forget that we still possess the power and the potential to change our own life and the world around us into an earthly heaven. Never should we abandon hope, even when we are struggling to survive in an ocean of tears. Five centuries ago a French priest and very wise man, Pierre Charron, said that despair is like spoiled children who, when you take away one of their playthings, throw the rest into the fire for madness. Despair grows angry with itself, becomes its own executioner, and revenges its misfortunes on its own head. We must never ever allow ourselves to contemplate this tragic form of suicide by giving up on ourselves!"

The old man shifted his position and gazed out the window at the nearby pine and birch trees. I remained silent. Staring at the trees he said, "Despair is the offspring of fear, and it comes to us . . . any of us . . . after we lose confidence that we can deal with life's terrible problems. When we reach that point, few of us realize that we are also admitting that we have even lost faith in God's ability to assist us. How wonderful it will be, Mister Og, when we have our army of self-confident, inspired ragpickers who will be able to rescue others from the treadmill of failure so that a vast number can make their contribution toward creating a better world. Well, they are out there, waiting to be salvaged from the dumps of failure that are everywhere . . . so let us begin . . . you and me. At the very least, perhaps we can light a tiny flame that might ignite the cannon whose explosion will signal the commencement of the overthrow of those terrible tyrants called despair, failure, poverty, and all the other plagues that threaten to destroy mankind."

Simon pointed to his papers on the coffee table and sighed. "I burned several large cartons of my scribblings in the past few weeks. Somehow, as I looked through them, they seemed to remind me of the thousands of currently available how-to books dealing with every aspect of our personal and business lives and every technical and scientific rule for managing and selling and parenting and living . . . so many books that if we tried to read and understand only a small percentage of them we would have no time for actual living and doing. As I sat in my little home and considered what I should deliver to you and how I should ask you to treat my ideas, I finally concluded that our most important mission, yours and mine, is to attempt to reach as much of humanity as we can with a very simple plan that, when followed daily, would give new strength and meaning to every life. Once people adopt our resolutions and make them part of a daily routine, their ability to deal with the challenges and problems in their lives and the world around them will have increased a hundredfold and also made them possible candidates to be ragpickers. Then, as they share our message with others, day after day, mankind's worst nightmares, from starvation to acid rain to the helpless aged and the many other terrors that threaten us all will gradually become little more than problems . . . with solutions."

He was taking me onto unfamiliar ground and I wanted to be certain that I understood. "In other words, Simon, you just want to pass on the key that will enable anyone to renew their faith and confidence in their own abilities. Once they use your key and manage to finally unlock that golden door, the rest is up to them."

Simon nodded his head vigorously. "Exactly! Exactly! That is a fine analogy, Mister Og. I would like you to look over the thoughts I have put on paper, decide on a simple format, and merely convert them into a brief but powerful declaration that can . . . and I hope, will . . . be read by the recipients each and every morning. If they do just that, within only a few weeks they will discover that the constant repetition of our message will be absorbed by that other mind of theirs, the subconscious, and eventually acted upon until self-esteem, faith, confidence, hope, and enthusiasm have been restored in sufficient amounts that any hurdle can be surmounted. It is all we can do . . . and yet it is also the very best we can do for anyone in need of a helping hand. A wise man once said that if you wash your cat he will never wash himself again. To truly teach your cat how to be clean you must roll him in the worst mud pile you can find. Then leave him alone and by the time he cleans himself he will be an expert at cleaning. The same applies to all humans. We can light the way for them, Mister Og, but they—each in his or her own way—must take each step. For those seeking help, that is always the best form of assistance . . . providing them with the courage and the faith and the will to help themselves!"

I must have had a puzzled look on my face because Simon leaned forward and said, "Mister Og, all we are trying to do is present some of life's most powerful and ancient creeds in their most brief and simple form. If we can teach people how to become more healthy, we can also teach them how to be happier and more successful. Recently, the Stanford University School of Medicine experimented with a program to educate the public on good health habits through the media, school programs, and classes in two California cities, Monterey and Salinas. The citizens were given very simple instructions on how to lower their cholesterol, weight, and blood pressure, how to quit smoking, and how to increase their physical activities. When, after several months, the results were compared with statistics from two other cities with no program, both Monterey and Salinas showed far greater success in all categories. Surely, if we can show people how to acquire habits that will reduce their heart disease rate, we can also teach them habits that will increase their success rate and they will be able to teach others, and on . . . and on. . . ."

"I'm ready. Now tell me, old friend, is there any particular format you'd like me to follow?"

Simon hesitated and then said, "I don't want to interfere with your creative talent in any way, Mister Og. Just let your words be simple, powerful, and few. For those we are able to reach, I would like our finished product to be their life guide, a beacon of hope perhaps, a set of directions that will guide them through the darkness for the rest of their lives."

"Simon, you said 'for those we are able to reach.' How do you plan to spread your message, once it is completed?"

He reached across the coffee table, placed his two hands on mine, and never hesitated. "In a new book of yours, perhaps? That way, with your readership, we will manage to plant millions of good seeds."

I could feel my heart beating, but I said nothing for several minutes. Then I asked, "How much time will you give me on this?"

"Take as long as you like, my friend. I know how you resist deadlines and I would not dare impose one on you. I feel so inadequate, Mister Og, since I certainly will never be able to repay you or thank you enough for your time and talent. Perhaps, if you decide to do a book . . ."

"Your friendship is all the reward I need, special man. One other thing. Have you given any thought as to how long this piece should be?"

"It should be very brief. History's most powerful messages have always been short and concise. . . . The Ten Commandments . . . Lincoln's Gettysburg Address . . . Longfellow's Psalm of Life. I would like the readers to be able to digest our entire message quickly, and I would like them to read it every morning, without fail, before commencing their day's activities. Knowing how difficult things can be in the morning, but also how important one's first waking hour is, try to write it so that it can be read in six minutes or less. Also, be certain they understand that it must be read every morning and that if they do as you say, their lives will eventually change for the better beyond their wildest dreams."

"Six minutes? Six minutes means some very tough editing," I said, holding up the notes he had brought.

"We have no choice. Give them a long document and they will lose interest, Mister Og, and without their interest they will make no effort to repeat the reading every morning. Repetition is vital in order to tap the subconscious, and you must make very certain that your readers understand."

"My readers . . . ?"

He grinned. "In the new book."

He had me. "Okay, let's set a deadline for completion. Outside of a speech at Hilton Head to the South Carolina Realtors next week, August is free of interruptions. How about the day after Labor Day . . . September fourth?"

"Excellent. That is a Tuesday, of course. Let us meet at the same time as we always have on Tuesday and let it be at the old pound."

"Done."

Outside the front door, Simon suddenly moaned and pointed to the dark sky off to the south. Curling up through the trees and across the distant heavens was the largest and most vivid rainbow I had ever seen in my life, and this rainbow, unlike most that usually fade at the top of their arc, continued in its sweep until it descended beyond the far-off hills, forming a nearly perfect half-circle. We both stood silently and watched this magnificent spectrum of color in awe until Simon turned and said, "Did you know, Mister Og, that science still does not comprehend all that it takes to form a rainbow?"

I shook my head and he continued, "What we do know, according to the Bible, is that after the Flood, God appeared to Noah and declared that the rainbow Noah saw was to be taken as a covenant between God and all of us. I like that. Whenever I see one I always feel that God is merely letting us know he still is standing by. Are you familiar with the English nineteenth-century novelist, Edward Bulwer-Lytton?"

"No."

"Included in that talented writer's body of work is an amazing paragraph that stands far above all his writings and it lives on, through the years, still graphic and wondrous. It is one of my all-time favorites. Would you like to hear it?"

"Very much."

"Mister Og, it also happens to be the best description I have ever read of what our next life will be like."

Simon inhaled deeply, threw back his wide shoulders, faced the now-fading circle of iridescence, and recited, in his best basso profundo voice, "'We are born for a higher destiny than that of earth. There is a realm where the rainbow never fades, where the stars will be spread out before us like islands that slumber on the ocean and where the beings that now pass before us, like shadows, will stay in our presence forever.'"

The old man turned and embraced me, then held me at arm's length as usual, stroked both my cheeks, and said softly, "Mizpah, Mister Og . . . Mizpah!"

Mizpah . . . and those special words, the Mizpah benediction, from Genesis, Chapter 31 . . . words that have always meant so much to me . . .

. . . *The Lord watch between me and thee, when we are absent one from another.*

XI

During the following five weeks I spent long hours, almost every day, reviewing Simon Potter's brief collection of notes. After clearing the top of my large desk, even to removing the telephone and answering machine, I arranged the various-sized sheets of paper from the old man's briefcase in rows that covered the entire wooden surface. Then, one by one, I would pick up Simon's notes, read and ponder his words, and often jot down my own thoughts and ideas on a legal pad resting on my typewriter.

Studying Simon's very concise observations on how best to change one's life for the better reinforced a long-held belief of mine, repeated in countless interviews over the years, that no one had managed to come up with a new and universal principle for achieving success and happiness in thousands of years. Many of the better rules for a productive life could still be found in ancient literature, fairy tales, and the Bible. For example, the "extra mile" concept from the Sermon on the Mount, obviously a favorite of Simon's as well as mine, works just as well today as it did when Caesar ruled the world.

Through his notes I was also pleased to learn more about Simon's very strong conviction that a daily repetition of one's plans and aspirations, along with a reaffirmation of the actions necessary to achieve those goals, was the most effective and shortest road to success. I had advocated similar methods and simple techniques in all of my books. One of Simon's notes read, "We all eventually become whatever our mind is focused on and in time we will believe anything we repeat often enough. Therefore, if we repeat our goals, desires, and objectives in the form of resolutions, day after day, they will eventually be transmitted to our subconscious mind and acted upon. The key to our success is to feed our subconscious mind, that mysterious other mind of ours, with the proper positive food . . . again and again. Man still does not understand how or why this surprising process is so effective, but centuries of positive results have proven conclusively that it is. Perhaps an even deeper mystery is why more individuals don't employ this powerful but simple process to help them fulfill their dreams. The only logical explanation is that they are still not aware of it. How sad. This is a powerful tool all ragpickers should use constantly. We still have so much work to be done."

The actual assembling of Simon's powerful words into a finished product did not take as long as I had expected. His elegantly simple phrases and resolutions needed little or no editing, and despite his proclaimed doubts about his own abilities, I'm certain he could have completed his project without any help at all from me. The wise old bird probably decided to get me involved so that it would be easier for him to convince me to

135

work it all into another book. In any event, the finished product was all Simon's, as I intended it to be, and borrowing a line that he had used in several of his notes I titled his complete work *For the Rest of My Life* . . .

For the Rest of My Life . . .

For the rest of my life there are two days that will never again trouble me.

The first day is yesterday with all its blunders and tears, its follies and defeats. Yesterday has passed forever beyond my control.

The other day is tomorrow with its pitfalls and threats, its dangers and mystery. Until the sun rises again, I have no stake in tomorrow, for it is still unborn.

With God's help and only one day to concentrate all my effort and energy on, this day, I can win! Only when I add the burden of those two frightening eternities, yesterday and tomorrow, am I in danger of faltering under the load. Never again! This is my day! This is my only day! Today is all there is! Today is the rest of my life and I resolve to conduct myself through every waking hour in the following manner. . . .

For the rest of my life, this very special day, God help me . . .

. . . to heed the wise advice of Jesus and Confucius and Zoroaster and treat everyone I meet, friend or foe, stranger or family, as I would want them to treat me.

. . . to maintain a rein on my tongue and my temper, guarding against foolish moments of fault-finding and insults.

. . . to greet all those I encounter with a smile instead of a frown, and a soft word of encouragement instead of disdain or even worse, silence.

. . . to be sympathetic and attentive to the sorrows and struggles of others, realizing that there are hidden woes in every life no matter how exalted or lowly.

. . . to make haste to be kind to all others, understanding that life is too short to be vengeful or malicious, too soon ended to be petty or unkind.

For the rest of my life, this very special day, God help me . . .

. . . to keep reminding myself that in order to harvest more ears of corn in the fall, I must plant more kernels in the spring.

. . . to understand that life always rewards me on the terms that I establish, and if I never perform or deliver more than that for which I am paid, never will I have reason to demand or expect any additional gold.

. . . to always deliver more than is expected of me, whether at work, at play, or at home.

. . . to labor with enthusiasm and love, no matter what the task at hand may be, realizing that if I cannot secure happiness out of my work I will never know what real happiness is.

. . . to endure at my chosen work even after others have ceased their labor, for now I know that the angel of happiness and the pot of gold awaits me only at the end of the extra mile that still lies ahead.

For the rest of my life, this very special day, God help me . . .

. . . to set goals to be accomplished before the day has ended, for now I know that to drift aimlessly from one hour to the next leaves me with only one destination, the port of misery.

. . . to realize that no path to success is too long if I advance bravely and without undue haste, just as there are no honors too distant if I prepare myself for them now with patience.

. . . to never lose faith in a brighter tomorrow, for I know that if I continue to knock long enough and loud enough at the gate, I am certain to arouse someone.

. . . to repeatedly remind myself that

success always has its price and that I must be willing to balance its joys and rewards against the precious piece of my life I must always exchange to achieve it.

. . . to hold fast to my dreams and my plans for a better life because if I relinquish them, although I still might exist, I will have ceased to live.

For the rest of my life, this very special day, God help me . . .

. . . to strive to fulfill the best that is within me, knowing that I have no obligation to attain great wealth or success, only the obligation to be true to the highest and best I can be.

. . . to never succumb to the fear of failing, because now I shall be looking up to the goals I have not yet reached rather than peering down at the pitfalls that always threaten me.

. . . to embrace adversity as a friend who will teach me far more about myself than any joyful run of success and good fortune.

. . . to remember that failures, even when they occur, are only guides to success, since every discovery of what is false will lead me to seek after what is true, and every experience teaches me some form of error that shall afterward be carefully avoided.

. . . to rejoice over what I have, little though it may be, always recalling the oft-told tale of the man who was sobbing because he had no shoes until, one day, he met a man who had no feet.

For the rest of my life, this very special day, God help me . . .

. . . to accept myself as I am without ever allowing my conscience or sense of duty to force me to live a life's pattern designed solely for the benefit of others.

. . . to realize that I must never accept the praise and love of people as a measure of my personal worth, since my true value depends far more on how I feel about myself and how involved I am in the world outside myself.

. . . to resist the temptation to surpass the achievements of others, since this pathetic and yet common desire is no more than a sign of insecurity and weakness and I will never be me if I allow others to set my standards.

. . . to ignite all my actions, both at work and play, with constant sparks of enthusiasm so that my excitement and zeal at whatever I am doing will subdue all difficulties that might otherwise slow my progress.

. . . to remember that I must pay the price in time and energy in order to increase my worth, for only fools stand idly by and wait for success to arrive, and now I know that the only chance to start at the top is in digging a hole.

For the rest of my life, on this day of days, God please help me . . .

. . . to do unto others as I would have them do unto me, to give more of myself, every hour, than is expected, to set goals and hold fast to my dreams, to search for the good in every adversity that befalls me, to perform all my duties with enthusiasm and love and, above all, to be myself.

Please help me to accomplish these goals, my special friend, so that I may become a ragpicker of value, laboring in your name with renewed strength and wisdom to rescue others as you have rescued me. And above all, please remain close to me, through all of this day. . . .

XII

Labor Day, which usually seemed to initiate the fading of summer in Langville and all of northern New England, saw temperatures in the high seventies, and the following morning seemed more like a brisk spring day than just another retreating step toward the autumnal equinox and the snows of winter.

I had made six copies of my final draft of *For the Rest of My Life.* After breakfast I placed three copies in a folder and large brown envelope, kissed my lady, and headed up Blueberry Lane toward Old Pound.

Simon, as usual, was already sitting on his favorite section of low stone wall when I arrived and stepped through the pound's rear opening. He immediately saw the brown envelope and exclaimed, "It is done! It is done!"

I nodded and handed the envelope to him. The old man carefully withdrew the folder from the envelope, opened it, and removed one of the copies. I forced myself to look away, into the woods, feeling like some insecure child waiting helplessly for the teacher to grade his paper with his promotion hanging in the balance.

At least fifteen minutes passed. Finally I turned toward Simon. He was still holding the pages of typed copy before him, but it was obvious he was staring beyond the pages. Finally his head jerked as if he realized, at last, that I was facing him and he said hoarsely, "It is everything I dared to dream it would be, Mister Og. Brief, certainly less than six minutes of reading time, and yet powerful. Sensitive, yet resolute. Wise, yet very simple and direct. If we can convince those who have lost faith in themselves and their future that they can immediately take steps to shape a better, more productive, and far happier life simply by reading these elemental resolutions and feeding them into their subconscious minds on a daily basis . . . if we can do that we can save many lives . . . and possibly our planet, if we recruit enough ragpickers."

The old man held both his large hands before his face, fingers extended and palms touching as if in prayer. "Bless you, Mister Og, this is a priceless gift."

"I did very little, Simon. The principles and the words are all yours. I just pasted them together as any good secretary would do, and it was a great honor just to be a part of your mission to lift humanity. I'm very fortunate."

Simon shrugged helplessly. "I wish I could show you how much I appreciate what you have done. . . . I have so very little. . . . I just don't . . ."

He paused, mouth half-open, his right hand grasping the wooden cross hanging from the wide leather cord around his neck. His eyes opened wider and then he raised the cross and cord up over his head.

"Here, my friend," he said softly, "let this be a token of my gratitude as well as a sign of our great friendship. Take it!"

"No . . . no, Simon. I can't do that. I know you've worn that cross for many years. It's part of you. I could never take it!"

"Yes," he nodded, "it is part of me. It has guarded me well for many years but I am really no longer in very much need of protection. Take it. Please. Let this small part of me become part of you, perhaps. And after all, it is not as if I am without all comforts. I still have this . . ." he said, reaching into his jacket and removing his old corncob pipe. "Another old friend," he murmured as he placed it between his lips and smiled at me.

I glanced at my wristwatch. It was just past ten, and I had promised my editor at Bantam Books, Michelle Rapkin, that I would be home at ten-thirty to discuss my next book. She was in for quite a surprise. I rose, holding the cross carefully in my right hand. "Sorry, dear friend," I said, "but I must go. Business. I'll see you soon. Thank you for this special treasure. It will be close to me as long as I live, I promise."

Simon smiled. "Nothing you could possibly say would make me happier than that. Oh, by the way," he continued, waving his brown envelope at me, "you have made other copies of this for yourself?"

I laughed. "Yes, I do have copies, and now all we have to do is figure out how to wrap a new book around one of them."

"You will," he said, "you will!"

We embraced again. I left him sitting on the

wall, his jacket open, once again reading his words . . . his very special words . . . and I felt very proud that I had made a small contribution.

Later, while Bette and I were having a light lunch in the kitchen, discussing my morning meeting with Simon, there was a frightening crash on the roof just above our heads. Within seconds I was out the kitchen door, looking up at the roof, and there he was, Franklin, the great blue heron, staring down at us.

"Friend of yours?" Bette asked breathlessly, her lovely brown eyes wider than I had seen them in years.

"Hey, Franklin," I yelled up to him, "glad you've returned. What's that you're carrying in your beak? A present for me?"

The huge bird nodded his head several times as if he were acknowledging my greeting before he opened his beak and a small object rolled noisily down the pitched roof and landed in the grass at our feet.

"Oh, my God! No! No! No!"

"What's the matter, hon? What is it?" Bette cried as she moved closer and knelt by my side.

I plucked the object from the grass and held it gently in the palms of my hands. "Simon's corncob pipe! Franklin has brought me Simon's corncob pipe! Dear God, something has happened to the old man!"

I stood, turned, and raced down Blueberry Lane faster than I had moved in years.

By the time my wife arrived at the old pound, she found me sitting on the granite boulders, holding the lifeless body of my beloved friend.

Later . . . many days later . . . Bette told me that I had been sobbing uncontrollably as I rocked Simon's old body gently in my arms and all she could hear me crying, over and over, was one word, "Mizpah . . . Mizpah . . . Mizpah . . ."